Show'em Your Scars

Robert Mattingly, Jr.

Tables of Contents

Dedication

This book is dedicated first to my Loving Heavenly Father whose grace and mercy never cease to amaze me. Then to my lovely wife, Gayle, who has loved me, supported me and at times carried me in my ministry. She also took my Southern speaking and turned it into a readable copy and for that I am eternally grateful. To my three children Matthew, Kaitlyn and Ashlee who have put up with me, Dad loves you very much.

I want to say a special Thank You to my parents Bob and Fay who brought me up in church and taught me about the love of God. To my Mother-in-Law, Freda, who without her expertise in editing this book would have remained a set of jumbled thoughts. Thanks Mom, I love you.

Foreword

This book was born out of a series of sermons, life experiences and the continual prompting of the Holy Spirit. When the Holy Spirit gave this to me I preached it once and put it on the shelf. I thought that it was really good and applied to my ministry at that time.

Two years passed and I was occasionally reminded of this series, but did not go back to it. Then after leaving my pastorate and taking an associate position I was called upon to fill the pulpit while my pastor was gone. I had five sermons to plan and I studied diligently, but came up with nothing. It was then that the Holy Spirit reminded me of this series, so I dusted it off and began to study it out again. Then things begin to leap off the page at me and the words I had written two years before begin to explode with new meaning and I began to feverishly rewrite the series.

I took five services and taught/preached this series and the response was overwhelming. I could not believe it, people were asking for copies of these sermons. It was at this time that the Holy Spirit said, "I want you to write these things down and share them with the church."

I put it off for another 8 or 9 months and then with the persistence of the Holy Spirit I began to put the series into this book form.

This book, I pray, is a wake up call for the church and a releasing agent for those who have great testimonies about how God has brought them through things and they came out victorious.

The scars referred to in this book are those experiences we go through that leave a lasting impression on us. Notice I didn't say a lasting wound because I believe that it's time we take the wounds that life has dished out and with God's help allow them to become our badges of honor.

My desire is to see the lost come to the saving grace of Jesus Christ and I realize that before you can tell them about Jesus they have to see you live the life you profess, share where God has brought you from and begin to Show'em Your Scars.

BUT HE (THOMAS) SAID TO THEM, "UNLESS I SEE THE NAIL
MARKS IN HIS HANDS AND PUT MY FINGER WHERE THE
NAILS WERE, AND PUT MY HAND INTO HIS SIDE,
I WILL NOT BELIEVE IT."
(JOHN 20:25)

CHAPTER 1

Scars Will Happen

In this life we live in so many things leave a lasting effect on us some are good and some are bad. Some are more noticeable than others. Some we can hide and some we can't. Some bring light glances and others long stares. Some we are ashamed of while others we wear with pride. What am I talking about? I'm talking about scars!! Signs that we live in a real world. Signs that just because we are Christians we are not exempt from living in a real world. Coming with life and coming with the things we go through we are going to endure some battle scars. Things will happen. If you are alive and have been breathing for very long you will obtain scars. Some of them we acquire by accident, some through our own stupidity, and even some on purpose. Yet with all of them come lasting effects that if dealt with properly can become badges of honor and if not dealt with properly they can remain an open wound.

We need to show the world what God has brought us through without giving the devil glory. How many of you have been in these testimony services? "Praise God I made it through this week. The devil really beat me up and I had to really endure things. I don't know how I made it but I've got another breath and I'm here today, praise God." And you say, "Oh my goodness is that the same God I serve?" We had a little lady in our church that if we had a testimony service (or as we call them now a praise service), this little lady, if nobody would stand up, would stand and say, "I would rather stand up for Jesus than sit for the devil any day." I'm not talking about giving the devil glory, I'm not talking about bragging about what the devil has done but I am talking about being real with people and telling them what God has brought us through.

Now I will say that in the church world we have been real guilty of glorifying sin in the church. We say that someone has a GREAT testimony. The person that used to be a rock musician and was on drugs, did all this stuff, maybe killed somebody, then gets saved, we want him in every pulpit in this nation. And half the time we hear more about what they did before God touched them than we do about their life after God touched them. We've been real quick to glorify those things.

You know what my favorite testimony is? For somebody to say, "I've been serving the Lord for fifty years and I've never tasted alcohol, I've never touched a cigarette, I've never..." That is the greatest testimony of anyone that has ever walked on the face of this planet. Because it takes more guts, it takes more unction, more character to serve the Lord like that than it does to say, "I was so far down in the pit that I was about to drown and God reached down and pulled me up." I am thankful He does that. But regardless whether you have been a "big" sinner or one who says, "I never have" with life will come hurts and with hurts will come scars.

I want to talk about the fact that Scars Will Happen. The world sees the church as either a bunch of hypocrites or a bunch of goody-two-shoes that have never had a problem in their life. That's the two opinions they have. I used to tell the kids in my youth group, "OK be a goody-two-shoes or what's the opposite of that? A dirty-old-one-shoe? Goody-two-shoes is not so bad." A lot of people drive by our buildings and look at our church walls, but never come in. Why?

Because I've talked to them and they say, "I'm not good enough. When I get myself cleaned up then I'll come to church. When I get things right with the Lord, then I'll come to church." Because when they look at these four walls they think the people are either hypocrites, because they proclaim one thing inside the walls and live another thing at work, or they're a bunch of goody-two-shoes that they are afraid to approach. I think if we are to reach this world for Christ they need to see some real people in our churches that say, "I've been wounded and I have some scars."

God is a God of second chances. I'm so thankful that God is a God of second chances and third chances and fourth chances and fifth chances. I'm so thankful He's not like my little putter counter that when I'm out playing golf runs out of numbers. I'm so glad He doesn't run out of numbers when He's counting the number of times He's going to forgive me.

God is a God of forgiveness and I'm thankful for that. But you know what? Inside the four walls of the church sometimes we have gotten to the point where we make people ashamed of where God has brought them from. I'll give you a quick example here: Let a homosexual come inside these doors and get saved, and get delivered from that hold the devil has on him. Then you let him come and want to work in the church and see how many people shy away from him. See how many guys won't shake his hand or hug his neck.

Why? Because we have said, "We're sure God forgave you, but we'll keep our distance until we're sure you're sure." I'm thankful Jesus doesn't keep His distance from me until He's sure. I'm so thankful that when I get on my knees and say a prayer He throws His arms around me and says, "You're forgiven!" Thank God that He does that and we, as the church, should be a reflection of who Jesus is. We've got to show them some scars!

Let's consider this and look at John chapter 20:19-29. First let me give you a little background. Jesus has been crucified and been in the grave three days; Mary has come and reported that Jesus is alive. Because of fear of the Jews and not really sure what was going on, all the disciples, except Thomas, are hiding. Fortunately they were hiding together. I think in this story a lot of times Thomas gets a really bad rap because he's seen as a doubter and if you are referred to as a "doubting Thomas" that's a bad thing. But I want us to look at Thomas in maybe a little different light and I want you to see something that each one of us should have. John 20:19-29:

V.19-On the evening of that first day of the week, when the disciples were together, with the doors locked for fear of the Jews, Jesus came and stood among them and said, "Peace be with you!"

V.20- after he said this, he showed them his hands and side. The disciples were overjoyed when they saw the Lord.

V.21-Again Jesus said, "Peace be with you! As the Father has sent me, I am sending you."

V.22-And with that he breathed on them and said, "Receive the Holy Spirit.

V.23-If you forgive anyone his sins, they are forgiven; if you do not forgive them, they are not forgiven.

V.24-Now Thomas (called Didymus), one of the Twelve, was not with the disciples when Jesus came.

V.25-So the other disciples told him, "We have seen the Lord!" But he said to them, "Unless I see the nail marks in his hands and put my finger where the nails were, and put my hand into his side, I will not believe it."

V.26-A week later his disciples were in the house again, and Thomas was with them. Though the doors were locked, Jesus came and stood among them and said, "Peace be with you!"

V.27-Then he said to Thomas "Put your finger here; see my hands. Reach out your hand and put it into my side. Stop doubting and believe."

V.28-Thomas said to him, "My Lord and my God!"

V.29-Then Jesus told him, "Because you have seen me, you have believed; blessed are those who have not seen and yet have believed."

Now, please, allow me to break this down. Let's begin in v.19, Jesus told them "Don't be afraid, peace be unto you." They weren't afraid of Jesus, they were afraid of the Jews.

How many of you know that when Jesus comes on the scene and says, "Peace be unto you." there is a peace that comes on the scene. In the midst of trouble, when you don't have a job and you have bills coming in and God says, "Peace be unto you" then all of a sudden there is something inside you that responds and you have peace. So many times when things happen in the church or people come in and they are afraid, Jesus shows up on the scene and speaks peace.

I want you to see something about Jesus—Immediately after He said, "Peace be unto you." What did He do next? He showed them His scars! The disciples didn't ask to see them. They didn't have to pry it out of Him. He immediately showed them His scars.

He's the Son of God. So the scars have to be an imperfection, right? Because in the natural world if you have scars on your body that's an imperfection. You don't think so? Have you ever watched a "beauty" pageant where a contestant had a big visible scar on their body? Or let someone who's been burnt terribly on one side of their face walk down the street and see how many people glance and stare and avoid them.

Jesus said, "I want you to see the proof of who I am. I want you to see the proof that all the things I've been telling you for three and a half years are true. Here's the proof!" In those scars was the proof of who He was. Even with His glorified body.

In my mind a glorified body would have no imperfections on it. Jesus was saying, *"These aren't signs of imperfection but signs of Perfection."* You must get that in your spirit, **"SCARS ARE A SIGN OF PERFECTION NOT OF IMPERFECTION."** Scars are a sign of a completed work, a total healing.

We're going to talk about emotional and spiritual scars. Some of you have some very deep scars and I'm going to challenge you to share with people the scars that you've kept hidden away because the church has condemned you over them. I don't want you to brag about them, but there are things you can share with somebody that nobody else can feel and you can say, "Look here, this is a sign of perfection."

Because of His scars His disciples knew it was Jesus and everything He had told them for 3 1/2 years was true. It wasn't because He walked through the walls but because they saw His scars.

If I was an unbeliever, you could tell me all day about the miracles that God has done in somebody else's life and I grant you that it might encourage me, but it won't necessarily pull me any closer to God. But if you begin to tell me about the things in your life that God has brought you through, and if you begin to tell me, "I know how you feel because this is what happened in my life;" then I can and will listen to you, because you have started to show me your scars.

People in the church may not need to see, touch or know the extent of your scars, but there are people outside the four walls of the church that do. They need to know.

In verses 21-23 Jesus gives them a commission, He says "Peace be unto you." By saying this He is saying, "It is I. Now you know these things I have said to you are true." Then He said, "Now go in the power of the Holy Spirit and authority I gave you when I was with you. I was dead and now I am alive."

Now Thomas wasn't with them. I ask you, why wasn't Thomas with them? I think he was angry and confused. We are always quick to condemn him, but I want you to think about what had happened. He was hurt. The preacher had let him down terribly. Tell me, when someone inside the church lets you down what's the first thing you want to do? You want to vacate the premises. The last thing you want to do is be with a bunch of Christians because they are going to be asking you to pray with them and if you do that you're going to leave there feeling better, then that "mad" you had all worked up is going to be blown.

Thomas was feeling a lot of things and I don't think that he necessarily doubted, maybe it's that he was just confused. He's no different than you and me when we get hurt in church. God forgive us, but the first thing we do is go look for another church. We want to separate ourselves from the people who hurt us instead of going and doing what God told us to do and that is to go and settle that account with our brother and then see if God tells us to leave.

In verse 25 the disciples went and found Thomas and relayed the message to him. They must have known where he was. They went and told him what had gone on, but Thomas said, "I need proof!" He didn't necessarily doubt what they said but you know what? He wasn't going to set himself up to get hurt again.

It wasn't necessarily that he doubted, but he was saying, "I'm going to be careful here because you know the old saying about fool me once shame on you, fool me twice shame on me. I'm not going to be fooled again so you've got to show me some proof here. I'm not going to jump off this cliff blindly. I want you to show me some proof." And there is nothing wrong with that.

Why do we have people chasing every whim of doctrine? Why? Because they are not careful to hear what the messenger is saying and examine it. That's why you have people who think they are the only ones going to heaven. I'm thankful we're not the only ones going there because I'm imagining it to be a huge place and I want company.

But Thomas was saying, "I'm not going to make myself vulnerable again if I don't have to." The world is saying, "I will not believe you know where I'm coming from until you show me." There's an old saying that says, " They won't care how much you know until they know how much you care." The world already thinks that we think we're perfect and that we look down our noses at them. We have to show them we truly care about them.

When the disciples told Thomas that they had seen Jesus why did he assume that Jesus would have scars? He was The Perfect Son of God. Why? Because Thomas had seen the humanity of who Jesus was. He said, "I need to see the proof. I need to know He's not a ghost. He's alive and has a body." Thomas was saying, "I've got to see those things. I've got to have the proof." And there is nothing wrong with wanting to have the proof. He assumed that Jesus would have scars because that would make Him the Jesus he had known for the last three and a half years.

Let me ask you, how many of you would be intimidated by somebody who told you He was the Son of God, died, three days later came up out of the grave and then showed up through closed doors? That would be pretty intimidating, but Thomas was saying, "I need to see that human side of Him that I've know for the last three and a half years. I need to know that this is the same Jesus that prayed with me, that talked with me, that loved on me. I need to know, and when I see those scars that will be proof that this is that same Jesus that I saw on that cross and that has come up out of that grave. I need to know that it is Him."

I love v. 26 because Thomas had begun to let his guard down. He had been in fellowship with the disciples and if you've known fellowship you can't stay away for very long. I have to assume that the disciples also went and searched him out. (And that is another book in itself about people that leave the church and we just let them go.) They had reconciled with Thomas. They had kept in contact with him because they knew where he was.

In v.20 Jesus immediately went over and showed the disciples His scars because for those ten that was enough. For those ten it was enough to just see the scars and to see where He had been wounded. It was enough to know that He was their risen Savior.

Thomas was a little harder sell and Jesus knew that. Jesus went over and He didn't just say, "See my scars, Thomas?" He said, "Put your hand right here, I want you to feel this, Thomas." See Jesus went to the one with the most need and He supplied the answer that only He could to the need that Thomas had.

We have people in our churches that we need to quit treating in "generalities". We need to find out what their need is. We need to show them our scars and minister to their need. We have in our churches today the greatest spectrum of situations, problems, and needs that there has ever been. We have divorced people, we have single parents, we have former homosexuals, we have alcoholics etc., etc. etc. They have been saved but still they need to be set free. We have all these people in our churches and we're still ministering to "Holy Joe."

I mean no disrespect when I say this, but Church was never intended for just church people, church is for the lost. Jesus was saying, "Let me show you my scars; let me tell you about them." People need for us to tell them about our scars.

There are some people you can tell them about your experiences and tell them about your scars and that is enough to help them. For some people you need to show them the things that have happened in your life and show them your scars. Then there are others who need to feel your pain and feel your scars so they will know that you know what you're talking about. You may have to expose yourself and make yourself vulnerable to things you don't necessarily like to admit to. But I'll tell you what, it's important at that moment for that person to know you know where they're at.

For all you saints who have been married 50 plus years, I applaud you. We live in a generation where that will probably be the exception and not the rule. You have a wealth of knowledge to share with young couples that are struggling with their marriage and are unsure of how to make it work.

But you know what? When there is a single mom that's going through a divorce, you can hold her hand and pat her on the back and tell her you know how she feels all you want, but you really don't know how she feels.

But you take the saint that's been through that situation and God has brought them out victorious. They can sit down with that single mom and say, "I know how you feel. Let me tell you what happened in my life. Let me tell you how the church responded. Let me tell you how God responded."

Do we want the little ladies that have been married 50 years involved? Of course we do! If I'm the one with marriage problems, I want those ladies praying for me. That's where the lady that's going through it says, "Ladies, I can't tell you the details, but will you pray?" And when we combine those prayers with the heartfelt showing of some scars there will be a prayer meeting that makes heaven sit up and take notice.

Here's the thing that really gets me. Some people will wear false scars just to make you think they know what you're going through. They are called busy bodies, but we won't use that term. But when you touch those scars and you really start to dig in, you realize that they are fake.

See Jesus said, "Touch my scars. They're not fake, they are real. In fact why don't you touch them real hard, put your finger in it?" Jesus said, "Thomas, I want you to take your hand and put it here in my side. *I want you to feel the depth of my wound.*" See this wasn't a surface scar. Jesus said, "Thomas, put your hand in my side. I want you to feel the depth of how I was wounded for you. I want you to know that no matter how many things you're going through in your life you can put your hand right here and feel the depth of my wound. I can feel the depth of your wound because I've got one also." Jesus said, "I want you to know that I know where you're coming from because of the depth of this wound I have."

Jesus wasn't ashamed of His scars. He said, "Touch my scars. Quit doubting and believe." Jesus was saying, "See my scars. Quit doubting concerning the illness the doctor has condemned you with, quit holding on to that. See my scars." "See them and believe. Quit looking at your bankbook and seeing how much money you don't have. See my scars and believe." "Quit worrying about those lost children that are running from Me. See my scars!" You hold on to that, because there are promises in the scars that He has. Those scars are a physical sign to us that He is alive and well and knows where we are.

Hebrews 4:15,16 says, "For we do not have a high priest who is unable to sympathize with our weaknesses, but we have one who has been tempted in every way, just as we are—yet was without sin. Let us then approach the throne of grace with confidence, so that we may receive mercy and find grace to help us in our time of need."

He knows how we feel. He's been through all the things we have been through. Some of you would say, "He's never been through a divorce. He's never had His mom do this. He's never had His dad do that. I tell you what, the depth of His wound says, "I know exactly how you feel."

When you go through divorce what do you feel? You feel rejection. You feel turned away from by your friends. Jesus was rejected. He was cast out by the very ones that two days before swore they would never leave Him or forsake Him. He knows how you feel and He's saying to you today, "Stick your hand in My side. Feel the depth of my wound. Because I know how you feel and I know what you're going through."

As Christians the world must see that we are real. Jesus wasn't ashamed of His scars and, in fact, they were considered badges of honor.

In v. 28 the light finally came on for Thomas because Thomas said, "My Lord, my God, you know how I feel. You've endured the pain." Thomas and the disciples were hurt and they were wounded and they needed to see that Jesus not only took the pain but that He healed the pain.

You might ask, "How do you know He feels our pain?" Let me tell you a story to reinforce this: I have a scar on the right side of my face where I broke my jaw when I was sixteen. It ran from about three inches below my chin all the way back to the lobe of my right ear. I had a motorcycle accident and crushed my jawbone. I now have a metal pin that runs from the center of my face all the way back to my ear, holding my jawbone together.

Because of that I had my teeth wired shut for six weeks (and my Mom said, "Praise the Lord.") When I went into the hospital to get my teeth unwired they had trouble getting an IV needle in my arm.

It took them SEVEN tries to get the IV in. I had people on both arms sticking needles in me. How many of you know that out of that I developed a little phobia of needles?

That was when I was sixteen. When I was thirty-five or thirty-six our oldest daughter was having seizures and we rushed her to the hospital where she was admitted for a couple of days for observation. My wife stayed with her the first night and I came up early the next morning to let her go get something to eat and to have a break. Well, while she was gone the nurse came in to draw blood for some test. When she told me that I was going to have to help hold my daughter while she drew the blood, I told her that she was going to have to wait until my wife came back because I wasn't going to do that.

Well she insisted and went ahead and drew the blood. When my wife returned my daughter who was three at the time was sitting up in the bed like nothing had happened and I was standing over the sink with a wet cloth on the back of my neck.

If that wasn't enough, when I was around forty my youngest daughter got bit by a dog and it nearly took off the end of her pinky finger on her right hand. We rushed her to the emergency room and my daughter was screaming at the top of her lungs, the end of her finger from the last joint was dangling by a piece of skin. The doctor needed to deaden her finger by giving her shots in both sides of her little finger. My wife and I were supposed to hold her down. The shots didn't take effect the first time so the doctor had to do it again. Now here I am, the Big Bad Dad, and I had to go stand in the corner while my wife held our daughter down because I was about to pass out. Now I knew that little needle couldn't hurt me, so why did that bother me? Because all of a sudden the pain associated with that scar came back.

I have to believe that my Jesus, who is at the right hand of the Father ever interceding for me, when He looks at His scars and He sees what I'm going through, He remembers the pain. He remembers what it was like. He remembers what happened. He remembers what it was like to be a human and have a nail driven through His hand, the pain, the rejection, and all those memories that come flooding back. I believe He remembers that. Why? So He can relate to me at that particular moment.

He's not some "Holy way up there God" that doesn't know my need or know right where I am. Sometimes I get in situations where the only words I can get out are "HELP!!" I don't have time for King James prayers like "Oh Holy God, Oh holier than thou that liveth wayth upth there."

I need help now and I don't have time to translate it. He's been where I am. He knows where I'm at and He can feel where I'm at because He has the scars.

If you ever need to be reminded of just how deeply Jesus was wounded for us I would invite you to go and read this familiar passage of Scripture. Isaiah 53:3-5: "He is despised and rejected by men, a man of sorrows, and familiar with suffering. Like one from whom men hide their faces he was despised, and we esteemed him not. Surely he took up our infirmities and carried our sorrows, yet we considered him stricken by God, smitten by him, and afflicted. But he was pierced for our transgressions, he was crushed for our iniquities; the punishment that brought us peace was upon him, and by His wounds we are healed."

He has the scars to remind Him! Sometimes when I pray, and we have all prayed, "Lord, by your stripes we are healed," but have you ever said "Jesus, I know you have scars, you know what this ailment is like, you know what death is like, I need you today." And Jesus can look at the palm of His hand and say, "I remember and I'm going to move on your behalf because I did this for you."

Thomas saw Jesus' scars, the pain Jesus had gone through, the fact that he was risen, and the fact that He was God and everything He said was true. Thomas knew that Jesus knew how he felt. Thomas realized what was in Jesus' scars.

What are some of the things that were in Jesus' scars?

1) In Jesus' scars was salvation, a reminder to the world, to satan, and to us that He couldn't go back on His promises, because He had the reminder always with Him. Death, Hell and the Grave were defeated and sin no longer had a hold on us. (I John 5:11,12)

2) In His scars was love. God loved us so much that He gave; His heart was pierced for and by us. (John 3:16)

3) In His scars was obedience. He said, "Not my will, but yours

be done." (Luke 22:42)

4) In His scars was healing. "By His stripes we are healed." (Isaiah 53:5)

5) In His scars are communion, a restored relationship with a God who says we no longer have to go through a high priest or through the blood of animals, but we can go directly to the Throne room of God, boldly go and present our petitions. (Hebrews 4:14-16)

In the Old Testament the priests had to kind of sneak into the Holy of Holies and the presence of God. They had to go through routines and through rituals. They had to fill the Holy of Holies with smoke to shield them before they could go in, and we don't even have to knock. We can go boldly right up to the Throne of God, fall at our Heavenly Father's feet and say "Jesus, help me!" In His scars, communion was restored.

6) In His scars was empathy. He not only can feel sorry for you, but He knows your pain. (Hebrews 4:15)

7) In His scars was compassion. He did it all for us and I am so thankful. (John 3:16)

In verse 29 Jesus commended the disciples and Thomas and those to come, not just because Thomas had seen Jesus, because he had seen the scars and touched them. Jesus said "My scars are proof to you, but blessed also are those who don't have to see the scars, but just believe."

He doesn't condemn Thomas for wanting to see the scars. In fact, He openly went and showed them to him. Jesus was talking about all those to come who wouldn't have Jesus physically to see; yet they would believe in Him anyway. We need to be Jesus to the world, because He's not here physically to show them His scars. We need to be Jesus enough to let the world see our scars and tell them what Jesus has brought us through. We have to be the hands of Jesus, we have to be the side of Jesus, we have to be the stripes of Jesus, and we have to be the ones to say, "Jesus had scars, and these are the scars I have."

Do you know what? God didn't love Jesus any more to bring Him up out of that grave than He does to heal your body. God didn't love Jesus any more to bring Him up out of that grave than He cares about your salvation. The scars on your spiritual body are no less important than the scars on Jesus' body at that point. He loves you and the world needs to see that we are not perfect just forgiven. They need to see where God has brought us from.

No, you don't need to spill out all the things of your life. But you know what? There are people out there that need to know that the church welcomes divorcees. There are people out there that need to know that the church loves alcoholics. There are people out there that need to know that children can find a safe place inside these doors and be introduced to a loving Father that will never leave them or abuse them. There are people out there that need to know!

They need to see our scars because they are not going to randomly come in the doors of our churches. Does anybody just happen to be driving by the hospital and say, "I think I'll just go inside and run around?" Most of us go there for specific reasons. Yet most of us will sit inside the four walls of the church and pray prayers that people will just come running through our doors.

Jesus is still standing with His hands outstretched saying, "See My scars. I remember the pain and I did it for you. Put your hands in my side and feel the depth of my wound. I endured them for you."

All scars come from a wound and in the next chapter we are going to talk about Attention to the Wound. We have a whole lot of people sitting in our pews that think they have scars, they think they are over offenses, they think they have forgiven "so-and-so" for doing them wrong, they think... but you let something come up, then all of a sudden that wound becomes evident and all of a sudden we find out, that's not a scar, that's an open wound that they've been nursing for a long time.

I thank God that when He heals He heals completely. I think it's time that the church rises up and becomes Jesus to the world. If Jesus wasn't afraid to go and say, "Here are My scars." If Jesus wasn't afraid to say, "I endured some things." If Jesus wasn't afraid to go and throw His arms around someone and say, "I know how you feel." He didn't care how they smelled, looked or were dressed. We need to be Jesus to the world. We need to be willing to pick up little snotty nosed kids and show them the love of Jesus.

My wife and I were privileged in March 2000 to accompany twenty young people on a mission's trip to Mexico City. We did four sidewalk Sunday Schools a day for a week. We worked in the poorest sections of Mexico City and it was truly a life changing experience. But one of the hardest things for me in Mexico City, but one of the things that blessed my heart the most, was what would happen at the end of each Sidewalk Sunday School. The little children would line up and they would go by and give us a kiss on the cheek. Mothers would hold up little babies that were 9 months old, 10 months old, and have them give us a kiss on the cheek because they were thankful we were there.

One of the hardest things was for me to grab one of those little kids that had snot running down their face, and as you mothers know, get a "booger sugar." But you know what I found? It wiped right off and the look on those little faces and what I felt in my heart far exceeded any repulsiveness I might have felt.

Folks, we've got to take the coats and ties off and get down to where people live. We are in the world but not of the world, but WE ARE IN THE WORLD!! (John 15:19; authors paraphrase) We still have to walk the same streets. We still have to go to the same jobs. We still have to go to those places, and we've got to be Jesus to them. In order to do that, they have to see you live the life you proclaim inside these walls outside these walls and when you begin to do that and you begin to show them scars they are going to begin to say, "I want to hear what you have to say. Tell me about it." We have to be Jesus to the world. And we have to be willing to share.

You know sometimes it's not easy to share because we are afraid people will think less of us. I'm going to tell you what, if I can share with somebody out there and make myself open and one person out there gets saved, I don't care what all of you think of me. That's not being rash, that's not being pompous, I'm just telling you that what the world thinks about the church and about Jesus in my life is more important than what church people think about church and Jesus in my life inside the church.

You have to be willing to show them some things because there are some things that I might share that some of you would shun away from me because of it. " Well, I thought he was a man of God." You've all seen this, men of God when some things about their past come out and all of a sudden they're not men of God anymore. Now they are low life sinners that were masquerading as pastors. Even though they had great healing ministries and many were saved and God worked powerfully through them, but now that we've found out something about them they're not men of God anymore.

Why were they afraid to share it? Because of that very thing. The Bible says, "If you don't forgive your brother neither will your Father in heaven forgive you." (Matthew 6:14,15) I think its time that we become Jesus to the world and open our hands and show the world that we're real just like they are. The difference is we're just forgiven and we're heaven bound.

CHAPTER 2

Cause of the Wound

II Cor. 4:8,9-We are hard pressed on every side, but not crushed; perplexed, but not in despair; persecuted, but not abandoned; struck down, but not destroyed.

Remember from chapter one that Scars will Happen. I want you to look at this verse with me,

John 10:10-(KJV)-The thief cometh not, but for to steal, and to kill, and to destroy: I am come that they might have life, and that they might have it more abundantly.

I'm so thankful for that promise God has given us. He said, "I have come that you might have life and have it more abundantly." You know, too many Christians are sitting in our pews and settling for second rate Christianity. They are settling for second-rate blessings. They are settling for second rate, what God has for them. He came to give you life and that more abundantly!

I'm sorry and maybe I'm going to get a little far off the deep end because I'm going to stretch some of your faith, if that's ok. I understand disease; I understand we are in a carnal body. I understand that things happen to this body. I understand that things happen in my life. But you know what? When bad things happen I'm not living an abundant life! When the devil comes along and attacks my finances I'm not living an abundant life. When he is allowed to attack my body I'm not living an abundant life. Jesus said, " I have come to give you life and that more abundantly!" And folks we are writing things off that happen to us as, " That is just the will of God." It is not God's will for you to have to worry and suffer; it is not God's will for you to have to worry from paycheck to paycheck. It is not God's will! He came to give you life and that more abundantly.

I'm not teaching prosperity and riches but I'm telling you that I can have abundant life with five dollars in the bank or I can have abundant life with five million in the bank. Some of you are saying, "I can have more abundant life with five million." Not necessarily, because I don't have to worry about someone going to my children's school and kidnapping my kids and holding them for ransom. I don't have to worry about all those things. I don't have to worry about paying Uncle Sam all that money in taxes.

As Christians, as sons and daughters of the living God, we have got to quit settling for second rate and buying into the lies of the enemy that say, "that's just the way it is." He said, "I have come to give you life and that more abundantly." Abundance or abundantly is defined in Webster's Dictionary as: ample sufficiency; great plenty, fully sufficient; plentiful, to overflow. If you are settling for any thing less you are not living abundant life.

In chapter one we talked about scars and Jesus sharing His scars, but in order for there to be scars, there had to be a wound. And so many people in our churches have wounds that they think are scars.

What is a wound? Again Webster's defines a wound as: injury; hurt; damage; to hurt by violence, to hurt the feelings of, to injure. With that said, there are many people that are so sure they are over something but when the least little thing happens all of a sudden those emotions rise up again, that anger rises up again, those hurt feelings rise up again, and they thought they were over it.

In reality they have a wound that they continue to nurse and I'm telling you that part of abundant life is living without wounds.

You can live with a scar, you can wear it as a badge of honor, but when you have a wound it is not a sign of a healthy body. You can't be a healthy Christian if you are continuing to nurse an open wound.

People ignore wounds thinking they are healed over but unless you establish the "cause of your wound" it will never truly heal. We are going to talk about "The Cause of the Wound". We are going to identify the cause, we're going to turn it over to Him and we are going to let God give us abundant life.

Unfortunately there are people all over that have a smile on their face, they shake your hand, some teach classes, some serve on the worship team, some work with your children, or about any other job in the church you can think of and they are hurting.

We have the impression that once you come to Jesus all your wounds will be healed and that's the way it should be, but there are too many good Christians sitting in our churches on a regular basis that are hurting.

Some have fresh wounds, some have running sores, some have partially healed wounds that keep getting busted open and still others have infected wounds that even the slightest thing can bring intense pain. Just like a wound in the physical, until you establish the severity of the wound you don't know how to treat it.

You have to understand that I'm going to use a lot of analogies regarding the physical, but everything in the physical corresponds to the spiritual. If we have a spiritual man and we talked in chapter one that Christ was risen with a glorified body then the things in the physical have a correspondence into the spiritual.

How many of you know that when your kids come in and they have fallen down and they have scraped their knee, you cannot know how to begin to treat it until you know how severe the wound is. Does it require a kiss? Does it require being cleaned out and a bandage? Does it require going to the doctor and getting some stitches?

Too many of us have wounds that we have been treating with a band-aid when in reality they need stitches. I want to talk to you about the cause of wounds. Just like the kid that doesn't want you to look at his boo-boo because it hurts so badly but still wants you to make it feel better.

You know when your kids come in, they are crying and they have their hands clamped over their knee so tight you can't pry it loose with a crow bar. "But heal it, make it better Mom" and it's not until you can get those fingers apart can you treat it. So many of us go to Jesus with hurts but we're keeping our hands around them and we're saying, "God make it better but we don't want to show it to you." Yes, God is all knowing but you know what? He leaves some things up to us.

Sometimes we have to pry our fingers apart and become vulnerable and say, "Ok God, here it is, here's the wound" and then God can begin to do the work.

What I've have found about a wound is that as long as you keep pressure on it, it doesn't hurt near as badly. We have a lot of Christians walking around with their thumb stuck on a wound and as long as they have their thumb stuck on it, it's ok, but you let some activity come along that jerks their thumb off and oh, man, now it hurts.

We have to pry our hands off of the wound and endure a little pain to let Jesus begin to see the severity of the wound. Even Jesus won't heal your wound until you allow Him to see the severity of it. You might say, "Oh God knows everything." Oh yes He does, but He's not going to do anything against your will.

We can never grow to the spiritual level where God wants us to be until we are willing to pull our hands back and let the Great Physician look at the wound. Now I want you to hear something here. If we believe that God is the Great Physician (and He is), and the church is His hospital, then that would make each and everyone of us who call ourselves Christian, His nurses.

The Great Physician may only diagnose the problem then He may use a nurse to treat it. How many of you have gone to the doctor and you sit in the waiting room for a half hour to forty-five minutes reading magazines that you really don't care about? Then you go into another room to wait for thirty more minutes for the doctor to come in and spend a few minutes with you to examine you and tell you what's wrong. Then what does he do? He sends the nurse in to treat you. You might say, "I'm paying good money for this, bring him back in here. Get him back in here to put this bandage on my knee." But he uses a nurse to come in and treat your wound.

We have people sitting in our churches that when they do pry their hands off and Jesus sees the severity of the wound He calls on a nurse to come and treat the problem. How many of you know that we have a lot of people in our churches that are not showing up for work? Let me ask you, "What would happen at your job if you didn't show up for work four or five days in a row?" Then you just bop back in and say, "Ok I'm ready to be used" and they say, "Good. Use your shoes and go down and get in the unemployment line"

God has called each and every one of us to be a nurse in His hospital. And if we will allow Him to, Jesus will come in and diagnose the problem. Then He may use one of us to treat it. Now sometimes He does choose to come in and treat the wound personally, but there are a lot of wounds in the church that if we would have a good nurse step up to the plate they could begin the treatment by applying the band aid that is needed. They could go and apply the ointment that is needed. Why? Because the doctor has told them how to treat the wound.

Too many of us are waiting for the doctor to come in and not only diagnose the problem, but to treat every single patient. That's not what the church was intended for. We have got to be the nurses in God's hospital to help treat patients. But we all get so busy in our lives that we don't have time for somebody else's problems. We have enough problems of our own. Well I'm going to let you in on a little secret and it's not going to cost you a dime. When you begin to give out to other people, your problems seem to disappear. When you begin to pour out into someone else and their problems, your problems don't seem so big. When you begin to give of yourself, you seem to forget what's going on in your life. I want to challenge you to be a nurse in the hospital of God and don't depend on God to do all the work because He's not going to do it.

If you know someone who's profession is nursing, ask them what would happen if they went in and told the doctor, "Hey doc, they want you to go in and put the bandage on their wound." What would the doctor say? He'd probably say, "Tell'em I said, I have complete confidence in you and you're suppose to do it." But all the time we see people in our churches, we recognize that there are things going on and we'll say, "God, will you touch them. God, will you bless them?" and we should do that, but maybe God is saying, "Hey, you go and treat that wound, you go and apply some healing balm, you go in the power of the Holy Spirit and YOU help them through it."

We have to recognize that the church has turned inward. We

have become turned so inward that the enemy has been able to divide us. We have become so turned inward that we are no longer caring for each other. We are no longer bringing the soldiers off the battlefield; we're leaving them on the field to die. We need to be more like the Marines that have a tradition that no soldier is left on the battlefield, dead or alive.

God is saying in Revelation 19:7, "I'm coming for a bride who has made herself ready." And part of being ready is taking care of each other. You might say, "My life is too busy. I don't have time for somebody else's problems." You need to do what God has called you to do and that's be a nurse!!

Back to the wounds. Sometimes it's just painful to admit that we have a wound. You know how guys are. Are any of you guys like me? My wife knows that if I say I need to go to the doctor, then I am sick. We like to cover those things up and we don't like to admit to those things and it's the same inside the church.

We think, "Somebody will think less of me." It's time we get over that. It's time we pull our brothers and sisters along side and say, "Hey, I've got something going on. Can you help me?" Because I'm telling you not admitting you need help is selfish pride. That is going to be a weight around your leg that will not allow you to leave this earth when the trumpet sounds.

It's time we join together. We think, "You know, they have enough problems of their own." Well, praise God, get together and discuss your problems and pray for each other, build each other up, lift each other up. In Ecclesiastes 4:12 it says, "Though one may be overpowered, two can defend themselves. A cord of three strands is not quickly broken." Let's bind together and heal the wounds inside these walls so we can deal with the wounds outside these walls.

There's nothing worse than seeing a hospital that's understaffed. I usually don't make reference to a TV show, but if you ever watched the show "M*A*S*H" there was some reality in when the helicopters would come in and there would be a flood of wounded. There would only be a certain number of people that could take care of them and some died because there just wasn't enough help. It's the same in the church. We have people lining up at the emergency door of this hospital we call the church and we just don't have enough people, enough nurses, that can take care of them once we get them inside the doors (if we get them inside). In the meantime they're staying outside the doors and they are literally dying spiritually.

There is no reason for Christians to live with wounds. One thing about wounds we must establish. **WOUNDS ALWAYS HURT!** You don't think so? Get a piece of paper, put your finger out and cut your finger with that piece of paper. How many of you have licked that envelope and cut your tongue? I have yet to see somebody slam his or her hand in a door and go "hum, that should have hurt." If they do, something's wrong.

Some wounds are shallow and they only last a minute and they only require a band-aid. Some are deeper and they need stitches and they require longer to heal. Some require surgery, something removed, fixed or replaced and they require still more time to heal.

We like to think that if we ignore a wound it will quit hurting, but what we are really doing is allowing that wound to become worse. As you well know, a wound that is ignored will get worse. Even when we have put a band-aid on it big enough to hide it, the slightest bump against the bandage will cause pain. You all know this; you've all had a problem, a wound; you put a band-aid over it and it looks real pretty, all nice and clean and everything, but you watch how you guard it because you don't want anyone bumping into it. You know the least little thing will cause pain. "Oh man, and I thought I had it covered up well. I thought I had medicine on it well." The same thing is going on inside the churches. We have people putting band-aids over wounds and they're walking around trying to guard those wounds and they think they have it hidden real well. It's up a sleeve where nobody can see it, but all of a sudden somebody bumps into it accidentally and the pain reminds you that you still have a wound.

Another thing we must establish about wounds is that, **ALL WOUNDS CAN LEAVE A SCAR!** I have a little scar on the back on my right hand. It's really just a little piddly scar. I was helping in a church hanging a suspended ceiling and one of the bars fell and scratched me on the back of the hand and now I have a scar about a half inch long on the back of my right hand. I thought it was pretty cool that I got a scar on the back of my hand in church. I was the biggest baby there ever was. I put a big ole band-aid on it, but it was kind of funny because it was just a little scratch, it was nothing big. But you know what? I did that about fourteen years ago and I still have a scar as a reminder.

I have yet to meet somebody with a visible scar that I ask, "how did you get that?" that they cannot tell me. And you know what? There are some scars that we have as Christians and when somebody says, "How did you get that?" We need to be able to tell them how we were wounded and how we were healed. How almighty God delivered us and brought us through those things.

At first the scar is vivid and the memory is vivid but the pain is not necessarily vivid. Reminders can bring back the memories of the pain but not the pain. Like I told you in the last chapter about my ordeal with needles and how it makes the hair on the back of my neck stand up, but you know what? It is all just a memory. I don't really feel the pain of them putting needles in my arm; it's just a memory that's real vivid. My mind plays a trick on me and says, "This is really going on."

A lot of times in the church we get hurt and we get scars. We let the enemy remind us of them and he reminds us of the pain. He even fools us into believing it's the real pain we had. In John 8:36 the Bible says, "So if the Son sets you free, you will be free indeed."

In one of the later chapters I'm going to discuss this more in depth, but it can only be painful again if you allow the enemy to inflict a new wound. Because if it's under the blood that old wound has been healed and has become a scar and A SCAR CANNOT BE REOPENED. If you were to take a knife and cut on this scar under my chin, which has a vivid edge, you would not be reopening this scar, you would be creating a new wound. The only way the enemy can get into your life through those things God has delivered you from is if you allow him to inflict a new wound. Once God has healed you and blessed that scar it is done with. God allows scars to remain as reminders of what He has done for you.

Too many Christians are running around with a cut spiritual artery trying to put a band-aid on it. You think about that in the natural. If somebody has a big cut on the side of their neck and they have their hand wrapped around it and they are just walking around and blood is dripping off their hand, squirting between their fingers you would say, "What's wrong?" They say, "Nothing, Why?" "Your neck, it's bleeding!!!" "Oh NO, NO, NO that's not really bleeding. I've got it taken care of. It's ok." You would think they were nuts!! You would almost physically take them to the hospital. But you know in the church we see people that are hurting and it's the same thing; they are literally bleeding to death. Spiritually they have their hand over their wound and we're ignoring it.

Too many Christians are putting a band-aid on what needs to go to the Master Surgeon. But we're afraid somebody will say something or somebody will see something. Guess what? **THEY ALREADY KNOW BECAUSE YOU ARE BLEEDING ALL OVER THE PLACE.**

Some people don't like to think of the cause of the wound, because they think it's less painful to nurse an open wound than to face the cause. But until you are willing to get to the cause of the wound, the healing can never be complete.

If you have a wound on your hand and it has an infection, someone can stitch it up and put a band-aid on it all day long, but it's not going to get better until the infection is treated and you get to the root of the problem.

Maybe you have a wound that you think is a scar. You serve the Lord faithfully, but down deep in your life, down deep in your heart, you are saying, " I wouldn't want him or her to get hit by a bus or anything but if they died tomorrow I wouldn't shed a tear." You still have something that you're trying to keep open and nurse along. You have not been completely healed of that wound.

Let me tell you, in God's hospital He doesn't have to run any test. He doesn't have to take you to the x-ray room. All He needs is for you to say, "It hurts here and this is what caused it." Then He can come in and do the work in your life. Also understand that He may use nurses to assist Him with your healing. So don't refuse the help of a good nurse.

Some of the surgeries that doctors do amaze me. They will have three or four surgeons in the operating room and a dozen or more people around assisting them. Those surgeons would be totally lost if it weren't for those assisting them, handing them the necessary surgical instruments. In this hospital of God, Jesus may do the surgery but He's depending on you and me to be standing there handing Him our prayers, to hand Him our beliefs, to hand Him our faith, to hand Him those things He needs to do the work so the job can be done completely.

The doctor usually comes in and sees you one time a day after you've had surgery, but the nurse comes in several times and wakes you up in the middle of the night to check on you. It's time we get over worrying about disturbing people. We must be determined to say, like Jesus said, "I must be about my Father's business." Who are you answering to? Jesus or the world?

Now, let's look at some causes of wounds: 1) Wounds can be caused by others, 2) Wounds can be caused by environment, 3) Wounds can be caused by family, 4) Wounds can be caused by self, 5) Wounds can be caused by the unexplainable.

1) Wounds can be caused by others:

This can be your friends. Maybe they let you down, took advantage of you, abused you, stole from you and you just can't trust again. We live in probably the most distrustful society there has ever been. People don't trust anybody. Husbands don't trust wives, wives don't trust husbands, kids don't trust parents, parents don't trust kids, we don't trust government, we don't trust pastors, we don't trust our employer, we just don't trust.

Most of it evolves from the fact that somebody wounded us. Somebody hurt us and that broke our trust and so to protect ourselves we say, "I just won't trust anybody." In reality all you're doing is applying pressure to a wound that the next time somebody comes along and bumps it a little bit, that wound is opened up and begins to bleed a little bit.

Maybe it was a pastor or a teacher or a friend, an elder, deacon or other person. Maybe somebody lied to you, cheated you, stole from you or broke your trust in the church. Maybe you are still harboring ill feelings; maybe you have a hurts against religion, against rules. I believe that, as the church, WE HAVE TO START LOVING THE WORLD WITH OPEN ARMS INSTEAD OF A BIG STICK.

I believe there are some very positives in the Word of God that you have to share with people. There are "do's" and there are "don'ts". There are things you MUST do and there are things you MUST NOT do. Those are things that we have to share with people. I think it's time we do like Jesus and throw our arms out and say, "Come on in, let me show you how much I love you" then disciple them along. Well it's easier to just give them the list up front and let them read it for themselves. It's easier to just give them the manual (the Bible) because we know they'll read it. Right?

How many of you, if you took a job and they gave you a sixty-six-chapter manual and said, "Read through this before you come to work tomorrow", would really completely read it? It probably wouldn't happen. We need to take people and nurse them along. We need to disciple them.

In this fast paced society we live in everything seems to be instant. Well I tell you what, this walk with God is not instant, it's progressive. We need our brothers and sisters in Christ to take us by the hand and walk with us through some things.

2) Wounds can be caused by your environment:

Maybe you were born into a bad situation. Maybe you were born poor, maybe you were born rich, and maybe you were born into an abusive situation, maybe an alcoholic situation, maybe you were abused as a child, maybe where you work they have taken advantage of you, looked over you, not appreciated you, lied to you. Maybe in school they picked on you. See all these things can cause wounds that we can harbor.

3) Wounds can be caused by your family:

Maybe your family caused your wound; maybe it was an abusive parent, maybe your parents were divorced, maybe you were in a step family situation, maybe one or both of your parents were absent, maybe molestation, mental abuse, or physical abuse. The list goes on and on. Maybe you were put in situations where you had to grow up and you feel you were robbed of your childhood. Maybe it wasn't your immediate family, but maybe it was your extended family, an uncle, aunt, cousin, grandmother, grandfather and these wounds are the deepest because these are the people that you should be able to trust the most.

4) Wounds can be caused by self:

Maybe you made some unwise decisions through rebellion, youth, stupidity, sex, drugs, or alcohol. The list goes on and on and on and on. The wounds are real and the consequences are real. We often try to justify these wounds or blame them on someone else; therefore we ignore the wound.

Until we recognize the cause of the wound it cannot be healed. Some of us need to point the finger toward ourselves. We need to say, "You know what? I've been blaming so-and-so all these years, but you know what the truth of the matter is? I had a hand in it too. The truth of the matter is, it was my fault too. The truth of the matter is maybe I caused some of the hurt." But it's much easier to blame somebody else. In fact, some people enjoy being angry with somebody else. It's a whole lot easier than pointing a finger back at ourselves. When you can go to the cause of the wound and admit it was self the love of Jesus is going to come in and cleanse that wound and start you on the healing process.

5) Wounds can be caused by the unexplainable:

You don't understand why it happens to you. A car accident, a terminal disease, a crippling accident, someone close to you dies unexplainably, finances fall through, you lose your job, death of a child. All these things can happen and create wounds. And, if not attended to, they can become real nasty.

One of the bad things about realizing the cause of the wound is that then you have to do something about it. And it is called forgiveness. You might say, "But you don't know what they have done to me!! I CAN **NEVER FORGIVE THEM.**" True, on your own you cannot forgive them, but with the power of the Holy Spirit coming along to nurse that wound, you can forgive. I take very seriously the verse in Matthew 6:15 that says, "But if you do not forgive men their sins, your Father will not forgive your sins." If He doesn't forgive me then there is sin in my life. So I take that very seriously and I know I can't do it on my own.

I'm going to tell you what, if you'll run into the hospital of God and let Him apply some healing balm, there can be forgiveness in your life and you can be set free from that offense. We have so many people being controlled by other people that don't give a rip about them. People that have hurt them and everyday they let them control and influence their life and thought process, when all along they are not even a thought in the mindset of the offender. It's time that we let the Holy Spirit come in and heal us so we can start to live some of the abundant life that Jesus promised.

Some people enjoy their wounds; they will milk it for all it's worth. In fact they don't want healing because they have learned how to play the pain to their advantage. "Look what they did to me. Help me, feel sorry for me, and excuse my behavior because of what they did to me." I'm not talking about legitimate wounds, but there are some people that hold on to offenses because they know that if they were to forgive, God might ask more out of them. God might stretch them a little more.

I used to love to do this to the youth in my youth group. I would find one of them that had gotten into a disagreement with someone else and they were just as angry as they could possibly be. They would have their arms crossed in that angry position and I would love to go and make them laugh. I mean I would just blow it for them. They would be sitting there with that look on their face, you know the one that says, "I worked for this mad, I deserve this mad, they did that to me and I'm going to enjoy this mad." And I would make them laugh and just blow it for them and all that effort and energy was wasted.

Well you know, we have people sitting in our churches doing the very same thing!! Their actions say, "I enjoy being angry with that person that hurt me; I enjoy holding that grudge; I enjoy being bitter." But you will never have the fullness of what God wants for you until you forgive and turn that thing loose. The joy that comes from the Lord far exceeds the joy you think you're having by nursing those wounds.

Jesus did not want us to live with wounds. He didn't die so we could stay wounded. By His stripes we are healed. That is healing of the total man physical, spiritual and emotional. Yes, I do believe that verse applies to the physical but I think it's time we start claiming it over our emotional needs; we need to start claiming it over our spiritual needs.

We need to learn to say, "Lord, somebody has hurt my feelings and there are legitimate reasons for it, but I need your help. You said, 'by your stripes I am healed.' I want you to heal me of this. I'm going to go to my brother and sister and I'm going to ask their forgiveness." Then you will be healed because of your willingness to forgive.

A wound is not a sign of a healthy body. Until we establish the cause of the wound, the healing can't begin. I Peter 5:7 says, "Cast all your anxiety upon Him because He cares for you." This may be painful at first because it means dredging up old memories; it involves examining ourselves and being honest with ourselves.

Healing cannot and will not begin until you get to the root of the problem. Good Christian people lay hands on people, pray for people, speak in tongues everyday and are still harboring a seed of bitterness down deep in their hearts. Do you know what I'm reminded of? When God allowed a "lying spirit" to go and be in the mouths of false prophets to accomplish His will (I Kings 22:22,23). I'm reminded of God using ravens to feed Elijah by the brook Cherith (I Kings 17:4) or when God used a donkey to correct and save the prophet Balaam (Numbers 22:21-35).

God may use you to accomplish His will, but don't think that because He's using you that everything is ok *if you know that there is something in your heart that needs to be removed.* If you have a grudge or hurtful feelings against your brother, something is wrong. You will never be used of God the way He wants to use you.

For some it means going back to things this week, for some it means going back to things from last year, for others the last ten years, and still others back to your childhood. You have to call those things out to the Lord for healing to begin. There's just something about the words coming out of your mouth and hearing them in your ears that is empowering. When those words go before a living God, there is a healing that goes on inside. There is a release that goes forth.

For healing to occur you're going to have to say some things that hurt. They're not going to hurt God, but you're going to have to say some things and your ears are going to have to hear you say them and all of a sudden you are going to feel the burden lift because now you have truly released it to the Great Physician. You might as well expose them yourself because most likely those around you already know there is a wound somewhere because you're bleeding all over the place. The only person you're really fooling is yourself because God already knows. But He's got the OR (Operating Room) on alert just waiting for you to admit yourself into the hospital and today the healing can begin if you're brave enough to look and to bring to the surface The Cause of the Wound.

CHAPTER 3

Attention to the Wound

There is no way to be alive on planet Earth and avoid being wounded in the battle. I'm reminded of a story of a man who was on an island all by himself for years and years. When he was finally rescued the people that rescued him noticed there were three huts on the island, and curiosity getting the best of them they asked him, "What are the three huts for?" To which He replied, "You see that real nice hut over there with the shades and everything? Well that's my house." They said, "That's nice, but what are the other two?" Again he replied, "You see that one over there on the left? That's my church, that's where I go every Sunday, every Wednesday." Then they said, " What's that other one for?" He said, "Oh, that's where I used to go to church."

If you're alive and breathing you will get hurt from time to time. Things are going to happen. How they affect you and how you deal with them reiterates the fact that scars will happen.

We have to remember that all scars start as a wound, no scar starts as a scar. Until those wounds heal you can never be healthy. As we talked about, a scar is a sign of perfection but a wound is a sign of an unhealthy body. You don't see somebody with bandages all over their body and think, "Boy they're healthy. I wonder if they are on their way to run a marathon." When you see a wound you automatically associate that with the fact that they are not totally healthy.

In the spiritual body if you have wounds that haven't become scars you're unhealthy. How many of you know that some of you have been called to run marathons for God but because of the wounds that are on your spiritual body you have to be content with a 2k walk. I believe for the body of Christ, as a whole, to be able to accomplish what God wants it to accomplish it has to become a whole, healthy body.

The body of Christ is also the Bride of Christ and He is not going to send a revival to an unhealthy bride. I have yet to see a bride, I take that back, I have seen one or two that were in a car wreck right before the wedding and were bandaged up, that went ahead and had the wedding anyway. But for the most part, when the bride comes to the wedding day she doesn't come with a big bandage on her face. She doesn't come with a nick here or there. She is beautiful!! When Jesus comes back, when Jesus breaks open the portals of heaven and comes back for His bride, He's coming back for a healthy bride.

In Revelation 19:7 it says, "Let us rejoice and be glad and give him glory! *For the bride has made HERSELF ready.*" It doesn't say He's coming back for the bride that He has put up on a pedestal and He dressed her and took care of her. It says that He's coming back for a bride *that has made HERSELF ready!!*

God wants a bride that can stand on her own, not to be held up by crutches, canes or wheelchairs, physically or spiritually. **A BRIDE THAT IS STRONG AND MATURE THAT NEED NOT BE SPOON-FED.** That means when we get wounded we should be taking care of those wounds immediately, so that they can become scars. We have established that Scars Will Happen and in order for the wound to begin to heal you have to establish the Cause of the Wound.

Now let's look at Attention to the Wound because scars need no attention. I am not a medical person but I am married to a medical person and life also has taught me that **HOW YOU CARE FOR A WOUND DETERMINES THE SIZE AND THE UGLINESS OF THE SCAR!!**

I have a scar on the right side of my face and I shared that story with you in chapter one. I have a pin that runs from the center of my face back to my ear that holds my jawbone together. I had a wound that started about 3 inches below my chin and ran all the way back to just under my right ear lobe. There were 50 something stitches in it. Over the course of time, the scar from that wound has shrunk and it's under the edge of my jaw so you really can't see it unless you're looking for it.

There are other scars I have where I have done stupid stuff and wouldn't leave them alone and they are pretty noticeable. Two really stick out. Like I told you, I have a scar on the back of my right hand that's really pretty ugly. I got it helping at church and I wouldn't leave it alone and it just got ugly.

I have a scar at the base my left index finger that's really hard to find. I hate to even admit how I did this, but I lived in a mobile home and it was very cold and one of the water pipes froze and burst. Now, how many of you know that it's no fun to have to fix a pipe when it's 18 degrees outside. But you have no water and you have to fix the pipe. Being in a hurry as I was, I could not find my hacksaw and I had a PVC pipe I had to cut through. So I went to get the closest thing I could find, a serrated steak knife. I began to cut through that pipe and you know what? It cut through that pipe very easily. It just didn't stop when it got to the other side and it went right across my finger. I walked around with my other finger on it saying, "Can I have a band-aid?" Blood's squirting out and friends said, "I don't think you need a band aid." I had to go to the emergency room and get four stitches in it. You can't really find that scar unless you're looking for it. Why? Because I went and had it taken care of properly.

In your spirit man, when you get wounded, how you take care of that wound in your spirit will determine the size and the ugliness of that scar inside you. With that said, I want to talk about "Attention to the Wound."

You care for a wound. You don't care for a scar. Some choose to keep on working and busting a wound open so it can't heal. Guys are the worst in the world at doing that. We'll get a wound and throw a band-aid over it and keep working and the next thing you know, BAM, we'll bust it open again. Then we say the smart thing, "I wonder why that won't heal." Then we'll put another band-aid over it and the first thing you know we hit it on something and it seems like it takes forever for it to heal.

Well, you know sometimes when you get wounded in the physical you have to take time off. It's the same in the church world too. We have people teaching Sunday School classes and doing every other job in the church that have been wounded through their ministry. Somebody didn't think they did a good job or they felt inadequate in doing it. Whatever the situation, they keep on doing it and they are ministering ineffectively.

I grew up in this thing and how many of you knew that when you volunteered to be a Sunday School teacher, it was for life? I mean there wasn't an out. You kept teaching and if all your kids grew up, you just moved up and taught their class again.

We never give people a chance to step back and say, "Hey, I just need to take some time off and be taught." There is nothing unspiritual about saying, "Hey, I'm hurting and I need a little time off to be ministered to." You can't give what you don't have.

We trust our family's spiritual well being to people who have been wounded in the battle. Why? Because they said, "I will." They get wounded and they continue to do it, but they are ministering ineffectively. It's hurting the people they are ministering to and it's hurting them.

In this Christian walk sometimes it's okay to step back and say, "I have to take a break. I have a hurt that needs to be attended to." Not many of you expect a guy who has had open-heart surgery to be at work the next day. You give him time off. If you break a finger most likely you're going to take a couple of days off.

Why is it in the church that when we get a wound we are expected to go right back and do the same thing again? We have to take care of those wounds because if we don't, they will never get healed and things just keep busting them open.

Then, there are those individuals that choose to ignore that they have been wounded. They say, "They hurt me, but that's ok. It's not bothering me, it's not going to get me down. No, I'm not going to let it." Then we will just ignore that wound and you know what happens to a wound when you ignore it? It becomes infected.

It's the same in the spiritual as it is in the physical. If you ignore a spiritual wound and don't attend to it, it will become infected. Let me tell you, when a little scratch on the back of your hand that didn't bother you for weeks all of a sudden becomes infected, it has your full attention.

I remember once when I was 10 or 12 and I had a mosquito bite on the back of my neck. Well like anyone else I scratched at it constantly. It wasn't very long until that little mosquito bite became infected and became a very large boil on the back of my neck. It then had my full attention! I had to go to the doctor and have it lanced. If you don't know what that is, it is where the doctor takes a sharp instrument, cuts an X on the boil then makes his best effort to inflict as much pain as is humanly possible. He does that by placing his very large fingers on either side of that boil and squeezing VERY hard to get the infection out.

When a wound gets infected it will get your full attention. Why? Because it affects the whole body. It will make the whole body ill if left unattended. When someone's words or actions wound you and you don't attend to it and you just ignore it, you can get an infection in your spirit that will grow and it will literally make your spirit man sick.

What happens to a person's spirit man when he gets sick? He flees or avoids the hospital of God that we call the church, with everything that is within him. I think it is time that we, as the nurses of Jesus Christ need to catch some of those fleeing infected people and help them admit themselves into the hospital of God. But it seems that instead we open the door for them and let them run.

You can't ignore that wound or the pain will get worse. Some wounds are just minor and they need to be covered for a while and then they're okay. You know most all bandages we put on a wound are breathable so air can get in to the wound. And at some point you remove the bandage so the air can move around the wound and aid in the healing process.

Well, you know what? In the spiritual it's time we start taking our hands and our bandages off our wound and let the breath of God be breathed on to those wounds and begin to heal those wounds.

Wouldn't we look silly if every bandage we have put on our bodies since we were little kids, were still on our bodies? We would have everything from Sesame Street band-aids to flesh tone band-aids and our bodies would be totally covered. But yet we run around the church with all these wounds that we've thrown bandages on and ignored.

It's time we take some of those bandages off and let the breath of God be breathed on them. Let the Holy Spirit come and apply the healing balm and get that wound healed and take it from a wound to a scar.

If you ignore the wound, regardless of who you think you are, it will become infected. Some of the bitterest people I have ever met in my life sit in our churches. They say, "I remember back in 19 and 42 when sister So-and-So moved my flower arrangement from this side of the platform to that side and she didn't even ask my permission. Praise God!! I can't wait until I get to go see Him just so I won't have to look at her anymore."

You know as silly as that sounds, that's very real. People leave churches because they don't like the color of the carpet. People leave churches because the pastor said something that "stepped on their toes." (If your unfamiliar with that term it simply means he says something that hits really close to home and sometimes it hurts.) You know what you need to do? You need to take the other shoe off and say, "Come get this one too because I know God's doing something in me if you're stepping on my toes."

If you come into church and the pastor only pats you on the back, you need to at least get something stuck in your throat and make it worth his while to pat you on the back. Because He's not there to pat you on the back!! As a Shepherd he is there to step on your toes every now and then. Probably more often than not. Why? Because God is changing us from glory to glory. How many of you know that we can't do it on our own?

Look at the life of Paul and tell me what God used to change Paul from glory to glory. Paul said in *II Corinthians 11:23-27, "Are they servants of Christ? (I am out of my mind to talk like this.) I am more. I have worked much harder, been in prison more frequently, been flogged more severely, and been exposed to death again and again. Five times I received from the Jews the forty lashes minus one. Three times I was beaten with rods, once I was stoned, three times I was shipwrecked, I spent a night and a day in the open sea. I have been constantly on the move, I have been in danger from rivers, in danger from bandits, in danger from my own countrymen, in danger from Gentiles; in danger in the city, in danger in the country, in danger at sea; and in danger from false brothers. I have labored and toiled and have often gone without sleep; I have known hunger and thirst and have often gone without food; I have been cold and naked."*

What did God allow to shape Paul from glory to glory? Just look at that list. I don't know about you, but I want my toes stepped on rather than being beaten with rods. I want my toes stepped on rather than being in the ocean, but God took those things and used them for Paul's good.

We need to expose our wounds and let the breath of God and the Holy Spirit work on those things. When you are wounded you guard that thing, but as it heals you become less aware of it and you don't guard a scar the way you do a wound. You forget about a scar most of the time but you are willing to share the story if someone notices or brings up the subject.

This book is all about showing your scars or sharing what God has done for you, but **WE MUST BE CAREFUL ABOUT COMPARING SCARS.** What do I mean by that? I don't want to give the devil credit for anything; I want to give God all the credit. We say, " I was a very bad person and God lifted me up." And sometimes we can get into the mode of saying; "Well God brought me from being an alcoholic" and someone else says, "Oh yeah, well God brought me from so-and-so and so-and-so." " Oh yeah, well God brought me from so-and-so and so-and-so." We have to be careful when we get into comparing scars.

I'm not proud of this scar on the side of my face. It brings back some memories of stupid things I have done. I will share if someone asks about it, but I'm going to make it as brief as possible. I'm not proud of that scar, but I'm proud of what it taught me. We have to be careful that we're doing things in the light that God wants us to do them.

It does no good to recognize a wound if we don't take care of it properly. I'm about to say something that might upset some of you. To say, "Just let Jesus take care of it" is lame. Wounds make you weak, wounds can debilitate you, and wounds bring you down.

Don't tell someone "Jesus will take care of it" unless you are willing to spend the time with them and pray with them and show them how to let Jesus take care of it. You have to be willing to carry the load for them when they can't.

Yes, Jesus is the answer, but God uses our hands and our mouths and our being to do His work. He uses us to do His work, and for too long we've been super-spiritual. For one thing, we don't understand a lot of other people's problems and when we don't understand and don't know how to deal with them we say, "Well, let Jesus take care of it".

How many of you just go to a general doctor when you know there is something seriously wrong? Most of the time you want to search out a specialist. I'm not going to go to a regular doctor if I need knee surgery; I'm going to go to an Orthopedist who specializes in that surgery.

We have to let our pride down in the church when somebody comes and says, "Hey, this is bothering me". We have to learn to say, "I don't know what you're going through, but I'm going to find someone who can touch Heaven with you, and I'm going to hook you up with a specialist that can hook you up with THE Specialist and we're going to get you healed."

Instead we let our pride get in the way and piddle around with it, with good intentions, and in the meantime, that individual is spiritually dying. Let's throw them in the ambulance of heaven and rush them to The Specialist and let Him take care of it. Jesus is the answer, but sometimes people need help to get there.

Regardless of the offense, all problems, all wounds have the same root and unless it is dealt with the wounds will never heal. Things will constantly remind you of it and reopen the wound. You'll build such high walls of protection around that wound that you will become touchy and grumpy about everything.

I have found that whether it is abuse, rape, incest, being hurt by friends, divorce, hurt by the family, hurt by the church, any of these situations, there are usually two responses that happen.

Either people will develop a real low self-esteem where they have no confidence whatsoever and they just withdraw within themselves. Or they build these high walls that say, "I got hurt and you're not going to come in and do it again." They build these walls of protection around themselves and they won't let anybody come in.

I see this happen in divorce situations, where husband and wife build such high walls of defense that they can't see each other anymore and all they are doing is throwing bricks over the walls at each other, because they have the walls built up so high.

These two groups of people are easy to find in our churches. The first group sits on the back row with their heads down. You greet them and they won't look at you. The second group has built up such high walls that they usually come off as "holier than thou". It is human nature to respond in one of these two ways and we need to be on the look out for these reactions.

Both of these reactions, if not dealt with, will kill you. You'll both lose your self worth and become depressed or suicidal or you'll push everyone away and become all alone. Then you will have to look for things to fill up the void.

There are people out there who are looking for Jesus to fill that natural void and are doing it with everything but Him. We need to be there to take them by the hand and help get the right medicine on the wound. When dealing with any of these problems, once you've established the cause of the wound, then you can start the treatment.

Regardless of the severity of the wound, the treatment always begins the same. In the physical the wound must first be cleaned before any treatment or healing can begin. In the spiritual it's the same. For the wound to begin to heal it must first be cleansed. **THAT MEANS CLEANSING THE HEART, MIND AND SOUL WITH FORGIVENESS.** Sometimes it requires a longer period of time for the treatment to completely heal the wound, but the treatment always begins with the cleansing of FORGIVENESS.

Let me just say something right here as a side note. For too long in the church we have ignored some things that need to be addressed. There is no shame in going to see a good **CHRISTIAN** counselor. There is no shame in saying "I can't handle this on my own." As a pastor, I have had people come in and tell me things that I didn't know how to deal with, and, yes, I prayed with them but I found a good **CHRISTIAN** counselor that could help walk them through those situations.

Sometimes people have let that wound get so infected that it is going to take some real serious counseling to get them over it. I have counseled with people for two years at a time and most of us don't have two years to devote to somebody. Why not hook them up with a good, and I'm stressing, CHRISTIAN counselor that can help walk them through those situations? Then follow up on them. After visiting with a good CHRISTIAN counselor, the counselor always gives them an assignment that week to work on. You don't have to know what it is, but you can help them be accountable and do the assignment so they can recover and get well.

You know it used to be that if you said "I'm going to a ... a counselor," that people would look down on you. They would even challenge your faith in God. We have to get over when someone says, "I'm going to see a counselor", we say " (gasp), I wonder what's wrong with them? I hope it's not catching, keep them away from me...We love you brother, we're praying for you...from a distance"

I don't understand why God doesn't all of a sudden "Poof" everybody, but I'm thankful He didn't do me that way. He has taught me so much through the things He has brought me through that only I can appreciate, because He walked with me through those things. I had to endure some things, but Praise God.

No matter what the cause of the wound the cure always starts with forgiveness. To forgive, according to Webster's dictionary, is to cancel, to cease to bear resentment, to grant a pardon. You might say "Pastor, you don't know what they've done to me. I can't forgive them." Without God's help that is probably true.

I want to look at the forgiving process. Once you've established the cause of the wound, here are some things you need to do.

1) Forgive yourself

It amazes me how I have read that rape victims, incest victims and abuse victims some how think it was their fault. "I did something to deserve it, I did something" and I think "Dear God, where is that coming from."

You have to forgive yourself for the healing process to begin. Even when it's not your fault you must forgive yourself. You might say, "but it affected so many people, how can I? I'm a terrible person, you don't know what I've done."

I'm going to ask you a real bold question - would you stand up and call God a liar to His face? "(Gasp) Well no!!" The Bible says, "God is not a man that He should lie" (Numbers 23:19). Hebrews 6:18 says, "It is impossible for God to lie." If you have asked Jesus to forgive you with a repentant heart, He has forgiven you. If you say He hasn't, then you are calling God a liar to His face, and God can't lie.

If God can forgive you for it, then you must forgive yourself. Romans 4:7-8 says that not only are we forgiven, but also we are blessed. If God who knows all can forgive you, you can and must forgive yourself or else Jesus died in vain. As the old saying goes, "God didn't make no junk".

Once you've forgiven yourself, then you must:

2) Forgive those who have caused the wound

If you can forgive yourself, then you can forgive others. You may say, "I'll forgive, but I won't forget". If you haven't forgotten, then you haven't forgiven. Remember, to forgive is to cancel a debt, to give a pardon. We are not to be doormats, but we are to be cautious without being cynical.

Now I want you to hear that. You can be cautious without being cynical. Cautious says, " I've heard that before and I got hurt, so let's go real slow." Cynical says, "I've heard that before and I got hurt. You're just like them, so go away." The wound will never heal until you forgive from down deep inside.

In a sense, until you forgive that person, you allow them to control your life; you allow them to hurt you over and over again. If they were allowed that pleasure once, why would you want to give them that satisfaction again? The truth of the matter is, they don't care if you're hurt or not, so you're just playing into their hands.

You might say, "but it's their fault." I want you to hear this statement, if you don't hear anything else. WOUNDS DON'T CARE WHOSE FAULT IT IS; THEY JUST REQUIRE ATTENTION.

If I fall down and scrape my knee, it doesn't matter if I fall off a platform, if I stumble on the way to the back or if I was going out a door. It doesn't matter; I've got a wound that doesn't say, "Don't go down those stairs like that any more, okay." The wound says, "Heal me, touch me, and give me attention." Too many times in the church, we try to figure out what caused everyone else's wounds. We say things like, "Okay now, let's figure this out so you won't do it again, because that was not very smart."

All the time the wound is crying out, "touch me, heal me, and make me better." We don't have to know everybody's problems to pray with them and support them; we don't have to know what caused the wound. They do, but we don't.

If you were taken to the hospital in an emergency situation, the doctor doesn't slap you around and wake you up to ask you "Hey, what happened, how did you do this?" They can see the wound; they start taking care of it, taking the vitals and all those medical things.

In the church we're too busy trying to figure out what happened. We have to quit doing that and start paying attention to the wound. Then we can help them answer the question, "What can I do to try to prevent this from happening again?" Yes, the wounded person does need to know what caused it, but not when the wound is open and fresh. If we take care of the wound first, it may happen again but it will be more difficult next time.

If you are not a Christian, forgiving is almost impossible. Our human nature and self-defenses won't allow us to forgive because then we have to become vulnerable again. To get a wound healed and to make your self vulnerable again goes against your human nature, but if you are a Christian it can and must happen if you have any hope of heaven or a great life. I want to give you some verses now:

Matthew 6:14,15-For if you forgive men when they sin against you, you heavenly Father will also forgive you. But if you do not forgive men their sins, you Father will not forgive your sins.

Matthew chapter 18:21.22-Then came Peter and said unto Him, "Lord how oft shall my brother sin against me and I forgive him? Till seven times? Jesus saith until him, "I say not unto thee until seven times but until seventy seven times."

Luke 6:37,38-Do not judge, and you will not be judged. Do not condemn, and you will not be condemned. Forgive, and you will be forgiven. Give, and it will be given to you. A good measure, pressed down, shaken together and running over, will be poured into your lap. For with the measure you use, it will be measured to you.

We all like to take that verse and apply it to the giving of our money, but as you read this you know it was all a letter and there weren't chapters and verses. So as I read the part that says, "for with the same measure that you use, it will be measured to you." Then you have to go back and say the same measure, which you judge you will be judged with. The same measure you forgive will be the same measure you will be forgiven with. The same measure!!!!

I don't know about you, but I want to forgive a lot because I need to be forgiven a lot and sometimes it's difficult.

Two more verses please:

Ephesians 4:32-Be kind and compassionate to one another, forgiving each other, just as in Christ God forgave you.

Colossians 3:13-Bear with each other and forgive whatever grievances you may have against one another. Forgive as the Lord forgave you.

God is very plain that our eternity is based on our ability to forgive. Let me ask you, Why would you let someone that has hurt you cheat you out of your eternal rewards? If the word says that if we don't forgive He won't forgive us and we can't enter heaven with unforgiven sins, why risk it? If you don't want to believe that part, at best case scenario, you will never be all that God wants you to be with unforgiveness in your heart.

I have told you that you need to forgive and now I want to give you some very practical steps to forgiveness from the book "Victory Over the Darkness" by Neil T. Anderson. This is a very good book and I highly recommend it. Dr. Anderson says it so much better than I can. If you will take these twelve steps and apply them you can forgive and live victorious.

Twelve Steps to Forgiveness
From: Victory Over the Darkness
By: Neil T. Anderson

1. *Write on a sheet of paper the names of the persons who offended you. Describe in writing the specific wrongs you suffered (e.g., rejection, deprivation of love, injustice, unfairness, physical, verbal, sexual or emotional abuse, betrayal, neglect, etc.)*

2. *Face the hurt and the hate. Write down how you feel about these people and their offenses. Remember: It is not a sin to acknowledge the reality of your emotions. God knows exactly how you feel, whether you admit it or not. If you bury your feelings you will bypass the possibility of forgiveness. You must forgive from your heart.*

3. *Acknowledge the significance of the cross. It is the cross of Christ that makes forgiveness legally and morally right. Jesus took upon Himself all the sins of the world—including yours and those of the persons who have offended you—and he died "once for all" (Heb. 10:10). The heart cries, "It isn't fair! Where's the justice?" It's in the Cross.*

4. *Decide that you will bear the burden of each person's sin (Gal. 6:1,2). This means that you will not retaliate in the future by using the information about their sin against them (Luke 6:27-34; Proverbs 17:9). All true forgiveness is substitutionary as Christ's forgiveness of us was.*

5. *Decide to forgive. Forgiveness is a crisis of the will, a conscious choice to let the other person off the hook and free yourself from the past. You may not feel like making this decision, but this is a crisis of the will. Since God tells you to, you can choose to do it. The other person may truly be in the wrong and subject to church discipline or even legal action. But that's not your primary concern. Your responsibility is to let him off*

your hook. Make that decision now; your feelings of forgiveness will follow in time.

6. Take your list to God and pray the following: "I forgive (name) for (list the offenses)." If you have felt bitter toward this person for some time, you may want to find a Christian counselor or trusted friend who will pray with you about it (James 5:16).

7. Destroy the list. You are now free. Do not tell the offenders what you have done. Your forgiveness is between you and God only! The person you may need to forgive could be dead.

8. Do not expect that your decision to forgive will result in major changes in the other persons. Instead, pray for them (Matt. 5:44) so they too may find the freedom of forgiveness (Gal. 5:1,13,14).

9. Try to understand the people you have forgiven. They are victims also.

10. Expect positive results of forgiveness in you. In time you will be able to think about the people who offended you without feeling hurt, anger or resentment. You will be able to be with them without reacting negatively.

11. Thank God for the lessons you have learned and the maturity you have gained as a result of the offenses and your decision to forgive the offenders (Rom. 8:28,29).

12. Be sure to accept your part of the blame for the offenses you suffered. Confess your failure to God and to others (I John 1:9) and realize that if someone has something against you, you must go to that person (Matt.5: 23-26).

After you have forgiven yourself, and you have forgiven others you must forget. If you don't forget you haven't forgiven. Also, if you've offended someone you need to ask his or her forgiveness.

You might ask, "What if they don't forgive?" Then your obligation is over; you've done what you were supposed to do.

Well what if someone has offended me and doesn't ask for forgiveness? Forgive them anyway. **THIS IS ABOUT YOUR SPIRITUAL WELL BEING NOT ABOUT THEIR SPIRITUAL WELL BEING.** Why would you want to let someone else affect your spiritual well being?

The forgiving person who doesn't forget becomes bitter and literally becomes an enemy of God because he develops hatred in his heart. In Galatians 5:19-21 is a list of people who will not see the kingdom of God and listed among those are people who have hatred in their heart.

Forgetting is not that it disappears from your memory bank because that is humanly impossible. Forgetting is if you have forgiven them and they were sick, would you take them something to eat? If they were naked and in need of clothing, would you buy them some clothes? If they were in jail, would you go visit them?

That's forgetting. Forgetting is not; I forgive them, and then avoiding them when you see them on the street corner. Neither is forgetting seeing them coming and lying down and saying, "Kick me again." Forgiveness is showing love out of your heart. To forget means the possibility of getting hurt again, but it also means being blessed of God.

3) Don't Enjoy the Wound

Some people enjoy their wound because it draws pity. It means they don't have to face their fears or inabilities. A wound will bring more pity than a scar. Some people look for opportunities to be offended so they can draw sympathy.

Again Jesus said in John 10:10-(KJV)-The thief cometh but for to kill, steal, and destroy but I have come that you might have life and that more abundantly.

Some people need to stop living in the mully grubs and start living a victorious life because you see living with a wound is not only unhealthy, it is lazy!

It takes more energy to attend to a wound and get it healed than it does to just protect your wound. Anybody can throw their hand on a wound and run around. It takes effort to go to the doctor and take the time to sit in a waiting room, to sit in exam room, to get to see a doctor so he can send in the nurse to tell you what to do. It takes time and effort out of your schedule; you might even have to take time off from work.

Some of you won't treat your spiritual wounds because you use work as an excuse, but you will take off if you get physically hurt. To attend to that wound takes time and effort. It's much easier and much lazier to try to just keep the wound covered. But I tell you when you do that, something will repeatedly break it open.

I want to ask you a question, "Who gets more honor if you keep nursing an open wound, you or God?" "Who gets the honor if you allow that wound to heal and it doesn't hurt anymore and you go around telling people what great things God has done for you?" How should we live our lives? We should live it to bring honor and glory to God.

He receives no honor if you are walking around with open wounds. Think about it. He receives no honor with you walking around with open wounds, but if you allow them to heal and become a scar they become yours and His bragging rights.

When God gave me that thought I said, "Wait a minute, you mean when I get wounded and I let God heal the wound I can say, look what God has done for me!!" At the same time God is also walking around heaven and He's saying, "Look, look what he let me do for him. Look at what I did for him, look at him. He trusted me," and He brags on me because I've allowed Him to work in my life. He takes me from a wound, to a scar. Let Him heal some wounds for you today.

You have to forgive yourself, you have to forgive others, you have to forget and you have to quit enjoying the wound. It doesn't matter at what stage you're at today, God wants to take you from bitter to better, from wound to scar, from defeated to defeater because God is on your side.

CHAPTER 4

Remembering the Wound

God is calling the church back to holiness and there is nothing legalistic about holiness. There is nothing legalistic about living according to "The Book". There are some "thou shall's" and there are some "thou shall not's" but we've allowed compromise to creep inside the church. It's time the church understands that the body heals from the inside out.

Your body produces antibodies that attack the wound from the inside out. You may treat and do things from the outside to aid the inside but your body has to be healed from inside out.

How is the Aids virus so capable of taking over a healthy body? It attacks and destroys the antibodies that give the body the ability to fight infections.

The church body has to begin to fight this infection called compromise from the inside out. Even more than that, it has to begin with each and every one of us who say, "I will live according to the Book, not according to how I feel or how I think."

Friend, I'm going to set you free from that denominational tag. I'm going to give you a new tag and it's called Christian, it's called worshipper of God, it's called Holy and anointed, it's called Redeemed by the blood of the Lamb, it's called Praise God I'm headed home.

The church has to get healed from inside the four walls so that it can move outside the four walls. Has anybody ever been around these sick people? You go in feeling good, but they begin to talk about how bad their life is and they start talking about how bad things are and if you weren't feeling sick before you got there you are feeling sick before you leave.

Well, you know what? There are sick people out there that don't need to come in here to meet other sick people. They need to come in to the church to meet healthy people. Then they can go home from church encouraged, lifted up and picked up. The reason they don't is that we're sick inside the church and we have to get healthy.

Does that mean we're not going to have problems? No, that means we're going to immediately apply the healing balm of the Holy Spirit when the wound happens. We are going to get it healed even before it has the chance to get infected, we're going to get it healed before it has a chance to fester, and we're going to get it healed before it has a chance to develop into an attitude. We are going to stay healthy.

We're going to get wounded, we're going to get hurt, but we don't have to stay that way. We can call upon Jesus and I believe He's the God of the instantaneous and when I get my feelings hurt I'm going to go to Him and say, "God, heal me." and He's going to say, "Ok, Forgive them." "I don't wanna." "Forgive them." "I don't wanna." "Forgive them." Then when I give in and forgive them, the offense leaves me and I no longer have to worry about it and I'm healed instantly.

We have to make up our minds, on an individual basis, that we're going to live healthy Christian lives so we can join with our healthy brothers and sisters in the battle.

How many of you would like to go into a battle with everyone wearing a cast or with everyone having a patch over one eye? (You would pray that the enemy doesn't come from that side.) No, you want to go into battle with healthy individuals. Why will they not let this old 44-year-old guy join the military? Why? Because the military wants healthy, vibrant individuals who are able to carry on the battle.

In the church we don't have to be old spiritually. We can be 23 spiritually and running this race strong and being healthy to go into the battle if we will allow the Holy Spirit to heal us on a continual on going basis. God is calling the church to become whole and healthy.

God is sending a revival and we can choose to participate or to observe, one of the two. I'm not being prophetic, but I'm telling you the truth, when revival hits there will not be time to get ready. When it happens there will not be time to get IN. When it happens there will not be time to get prepared because it is going to be the revival that is going to usher in the Second Coming of our Lord and Savior and we're going to go "meet Him in the air and so shall we ever be with the Lord." (I Thessalonians 4:13-18)

There's not going to be time to get ready. You're either going to be ready and be caught by the torrent of the river of God as it comes through because you're ready to jump in, or you're going to be standing on the bank wishing you could. God is saying, "Get ready, get ready."

I've been hearing that Jesus is coming again since I was, as they say, "knee high to a grasshopper", but you know what, as I talk to my brothers and sisters from other denominations, our conversation always seems to turn to, "He's coming soon."

He's coming for a bride that is ready; He doesn't care what name is over the door, what denomination, what tag you wear. As I heard one preacher say about denominational tags, "they are either going to fall off on the way up or burn off on the way down." There will be no denominations in eternity!

In the last chapter we talked about the healing process: Attention to the Wound and now I want to talk to you about Remembering the Wound.

We are going to talk about how to deal with the healing process, but for the final healing to occur we must consider the Reminders of the Wound. Sometimes we can't help being wounded and sometimes we can. But like we talked about in the last chapter, the wound doesn't care about the cause of the wound it just needs attention.

If you have not heard anything else I have said in this book, I want you to hear this: **A WOUND DOES NOT CARE ABOUT THE CAUSE IT JUST NEEDS ATTENTION.**

Too many times we are too busy pointing fingers trying to

figure out who's fault it is, because we know it's not ours, instead of just taking care of the wound and getting it healed so we can move forward with what God has called us to do.

In the last chapter we talked about forgiveness, forgiving ourselves, forgiving others, forgetting, and not enjoying the wound. It's real easy in the spiritual, just like in the natural, that as a wound begins to heal and we can begin to do a little more and a little more we tend to want to over-do it too soon and usually we pay for it.

I want you to hear what I have to say because I believe you can relate to this. As God begins to heal that wound it's very important that you get back involved in what is going on. If you get hurt by someone in the choir and you sat out there recuperating for a few months and you've finally forgiven whoever it was, it's time to start moving back in. Maybe you only come and sing on Sunday mornings or maybe you only come and sing on Sunday nights, maybe you just need to ease back into it. You don't need to jump back up there and start singing a special right off the bat.

I remember a few years ago when my dad had heart surgery. It is just a terrifying thought to have somebody cut your chest open, pry it apart and set your heart on a table. That's just a horrifying thought to me, but I do remember that the next day they got my dad up walking. I hurt more than he did I think, just watching him walk.

If you've had surgery you have a stay at the hospital before you go home. For the first week you are at home you feel terrible, it hurts to sit, it hurts to lie, it hurts to stand, it hurts to cough, and it even hurts to breathe.

I remember that after my Dad's surgery, they gave him a pillow and they told him, "If you dare think you're going to cough, pull this to your chest as hard as you can, otherwise you will break your incision open."

Then the next week goes by and you maybe go to the kitchen by yourself. Another week goes by and you're getting around pretty good. Then week-by-week you get a little better. By week five or six you're feeling great. You go to the doctor and you tell him you're feeling great and he says "that's great, BUT..." Then he gives you a list of "don't do's." Don't bend over and pick up anything over twenty pounds, don't do this, don't do that. But you're thinking, "I feel great. I don't understand this, I'm feeling great." But the doctor is saying, "Don't do! You're healing well, but don't do."

So you go home and being the active person that you are you can't stand it and you're out walking around in the yard and you notice that the big storm that kept you awake all night has blown a big limb down in the yard. Well, you don't want to call and bother anyone with it because it's just a limb and you've been cleaning up your yard all your life. So, you go over and you pick up that limb. Then all of a sudden "POP" and you feel something in your chest give way and you hit the ground.

They call 911 and the ambulance comes and gets you and they take you to the hospital and the doctor says, "You pulled a muscle loose inside your chest. You shouldn't have been doing that." Now you're out for another five or six weeks.

In the natural we can understand that, in the natural we can understand that you don't need to do things when the doctor tells you not to do them.

Now let's relate that to the spiritual. Depending on the extent of your wound, and only you and God know the extent of your wound, sometimes when you've been wounded don't jump back in too quickly. You have got to hear that and if you've got a servant's heart, that's the most difficult thing in the world for you to do because you want to do something.

But I have also found that those who jump in too quickly are more apt to get hurt again, and the second time is going to be worse than the first time, and in many cases it drives them out of the church and we never see them again.

Now does that mean that we make them sit on the pew and do nothing? No, It means that we allow them time to ease their way back in, just like in the physical. It's the same way in the spiritual.

I taught the High School Sunday School class for nine years. A couple of reasons I did that was that I guarded my kids very closely. I wouldn't let just anybody come teach them unless I knew them personally and they had to have my personal stamp of approval before I would allow them to teach my class. I did take one year off to be a Sunday School Superintendent and I took another year off because I said, "I have to take some time off. I have to sit back and be ministered to for a while."

But you know sometimes in the church we look at wanting to take a break as a sign of weakness or we think, "They must be slipping. They must be slipping into sin, something must be wrong in their life."

In the church let's quit looking at the negative. The world keeps pointing fingers at you seven days a week. Statistics say that for every one negative you receive, you need seven positives to erase that negative. The church should be a positive place. We should want to believe the good about people. We should want to believe the positive things about people. People should be able to come in here and say, "Hey, I want to take a little break." And we should say, "Praise God that you acknowledge that and we're going to pray with you and support you. When you're ready to step back in let us know and we'll ease you back into it. Because we believe in who you are and God has His hand on your life." Instead of pulling them aside and saying, "Ok, what's wrong, what's going on, how long are you going to be out? I hope I can find someone to fill your spot." Sometimes we have to acknowledge that we just need to take a break.

But by the same token there is a fine line, just like in the physical, between taking time off and quitting. How many of you have known people that have gotten well but they are used to sitting at the house? They are so used to just sitting there and doing nothing. In fact, they are really enjoying it and it takes somebody to come along and say it's time you get off the couch and get to work. In the spiritual we may not say that to them, but you know sometimes when they sit for so long it becomes comfortable to just sit there. We have to recognize that healthy people don't just sit around and do nothing.

How many of you know it's a lot easier to be ministered to than to minister? It's a whole lot easier to warm that pew than it is to actually get out and give of yourself. So let me just say this, it's ok to take a break and relax sometimes, but know when you have been on break long enough. And know when it's time to get back into the swing of it. Ease yourself back into what you need to do to serve

God and get yourself up and running so you can be healthy.

That's what this book is all about, finding the things in your life that are keeping you from being healthy and being everything God wants you to be.

I don't see anywhere that the writer of Hebrews refers to his Christian life as a walk. We often refer to our Christian life as a "walk", but the writer of Hebrews said, "Therefore, since we are surrounded by such a great cloud of witnesses, let us throw off everything that hinders and the sin that so easily entangles, and *let us run* with perseverance the race marked out for us. (Hebrews 12:1 emphasis added)" He said, "Let us run this race", so we can't be content to walk, but sometimes it's ok to step to the sideline go into the medical tent, get healthy, so you can step back on the race track and hit it full speed.

There is no shame in saying, "I just need to take a little break." Just like there is no shame in saying, "Will you help me?" We have got to get over that fear; you know "pride goes before destruction, a haughty spirit before a fall." (Proverbs 16:18)

Why is it inside the church, where we are suppose to be humble, and we're suppose to be helpful that we are the most prideful people on the face of the planet? UHH, I AM NOT PROUD. Oh yeah, what happened to you this week? Tell me about something you need help with that happened to you this week. You might say, "Oh well, it's not that important." Then I will have to ask, "Did it get you down?" "Oh well, maybe." "Did it pull you away from your communion with God?" "Well you know I'm busy."

See pride says, "I can't share with my brother." And, men, we are really bad about this and we need each other now more than ever. Church, we need each other more than ever, each and every one of us. We need to support each other with prayer. We need to pray daily for our families, our churches, our pastors and the list goes on.

Men, we should be supplying the prayer covering for our families. I pray two things over my daughters every day: I pray for God to protect them from harm, protect them from physical harm because I want to tell you that if the devil can't get to them spiritually he will harm them physically.

You might say, "Oh, he can't do that!" "Oh yes, he can." How can he walk into Columbine High School with a semi-automatic weapon and place it to a young lady's head that believed in God and pull the trigger? Don't tell me he can't, because he can. "Lord, protect my daughters physically from harm."

Then I pray, protect them from evil. Protect them from the evil of the world that comes everyday in influxes that say, "This is ok. Everybody's doing it. You're weird if you don't. You have to do this. It's weird to be a Christian." All those things that come into their minds. They need my prayers prayed over them.

God calls us to forgive and to forget but also to be wise. God calls us to forgive and to forget, and I hope you will forgive me for using this word, but that does not mean to be stupid, but to be careful.

Let me give you an example: if you've been hurt in a relationship and time has passed, don't let loneliness convince you that you're over that hurt when you know you really aren't. Unless you know for sure, don't let loneliness put pressure on that wound and force you into another relationship that you really don't want to be in because you've never recovered from the other one. This happens way too often.

If you've been hurt in a relationship, don't let loneliness make you believe you're healed and ready to try again because in reality your wound may be throbbing because of the irritation called loneliness and what you really need is a sedative from the Lord called the Word of God or a good Christian friend to relieve the pain for a while longer while the wound continues to heal.

You might say, "How do I know when the wound is healed?" *When pressure is applied to it and it no longer hurts. It may make you uncomfortable but it no longer hurts.* When someone has abused you and you can think about that person without reliving that experience or the pain or wanting revenge on that person. When someone hurts you and you can pray blessings on that person and mean it! That is when the wound is truly healed.

Does that mean that if I still get angry with that person I'm not healed? Not necessarily, because, for instance, in a divorce situation, you can forgive, forget and pray for that person but through circumstances beyond your control, that person continually looks for new ways to annoy you. So you get angry with them. Does that mean that you still have an open wound? Not necessarily. Maybe that person is just a jerk. Let's just be real. You would feel the same way about any other annoying person that did the same thing. That doesn't necessarily mean that you're harboring hurts. It just means that you are normal. OK, you're just normal.

I'm going to talk briefly about remembering. Not about remembering the offense but remembering the lesson that we learned. We must try to avoid being hurt the same way, but as a Christian you will be susceptible to hurts. I'm talking about hurts that you can't avoid.

I Timothy 1:15-17-"Here's a trustworthy saying and deserves full acceptance: Jesus Christ came into the world to save sinners of whom I am the worst. But for that very reason I was shown mercy so that in me the worst of sinners, Christ Jesus might display His unlimited patience as an example for those who believe on Him and receive eternal life. Now to the King eternal, immortal, invisible, the only God be honor and glory forever and ever amen."

I love that passage of scripture. Paul says in verse 15 that Jesus came to save sinners of whom he was the worst. The man who wrote most of the New Testament, the man who argued Christ before kings and authorities, the man who was imprisoned for the cause of Christ says that he was the worst of sinners. If that is true they haven't created a word to describe me yet.

I have to ask myself, "Where did he come up with that?" I think it was because he was remembering some wounds. Don't you think that satan reminded him of how he used to persecute the Christians? Don't you think that Paul played over and over in his mind the stoning of Stephen? Don't you think that he cried many nights by himself as he was thinking of how he was standing holding the garments of the ones that were stoning Stephen? I know he did! Why? Because he was man just like you and me and satan made sure that he remembered those things. He made sure that those things were brought up.

Paul would think over those wounds. Don't you think that he remembered the hatred he had in his heart for Christians in the name of the Church? Sure he remembered those things and I'm sure they saddened him at times but he realized, as we must, that remembering those things kept him from returning. Remembering the hatred he had for Christians kept his love for God alive. Not out of guilt or obligation, but out of a true love for God. Remembering how he stood and held the garments while Stephen was being stoned kept him in the chains, kept him in the jailhouse. Remembering those things kept him there.

We have to remember sometimes what God has done for us. You know some of us were so bad that we want to forget all of it. I don't believe in giving the devil glory for anything, but you know what? Sometimes I have to go and sit down by myself and begin to weep and say, "God, I remember what I was like, I remember the person I was, I remember."

I'm remembering the wounds that I had, but I'm also remembering the grace of God that reached down and looked beyond my faults and saw my need. Sometimes we get so spiritual that we forget where we came from. We are so content with who we are, where we are, or who we think we are, but sometimes we need to go back and remember.

You might say, "I've been a Christian all my life and I've never done any of that stuff." Praise God, look around you and see the trouble people are having in their lives because they have and give God glory that you've never had to go through any of that. Give God glory that you've never had to deal with any of that!

I would give anything if I could go back and erase some of the things I've done, but I can't. But I can look forward to the fact that God redeemed me from those things and look to where He is taking me. Paul says in verse 16. "That is who he was but he no longer is and though that makes him sad, he can't change it. But because in him is the witness that if Jesus can love and change him as bad as he was, look what He can do for us." (Authors paraphrase)

If God looked down on me and did within me what He did, I'm telling you that there is nobody out there that He can't save, deliver, bring forth, and set on the rock to stay.

He's my God and He's my Savior. He picked me up out of a miry pit. If I shared with some of you where God has brought me from you would never listen to another word I had to say, because you would not be able to see what God has done in me. All you would be able to see would be what I was before. That's just honest. So there are things I choose not to share with some people.

But there are some of you reading this today that have some hurts that I could tell you that I've been there and you would know and believe, I've been there. I know some of those pains and some of those hurts that you have and if you'll share with me I'll share enough with you to let you know I know how you feel and together we'll raise our hands up to a loving, forgiving God. We'll see you go from defeated to defeater, from broken to fixed, from unhealthy to healthy, from afraid to witness to a soul winner that hell fears.

My goal in life is not to be famous, my goal in life is not to be a great preacher, and my goal in life is not to be rich. You know what my goal in life is? My goal in life is that when my eyes pop open in the morning time, hell says, "Oh no, he's awake." When I step out and my feet hit the ground hell says, "Oh no, let's stay out of his path. Here comes that God fearing, Holy Spirit filled believer that's going to talk to somebody about Jesus today." That's my goal in life. I don't look for the accolades of man. I'm looking for my name to be written on the dotted line one of these days when I get to heaven.

Jesus is not going to have any trouble recognizing me because we've talked on a continual daily basis. He knows me on a first name basis. He will be able to call out "Robert," and there may be millions of Roberts in heaven, but I'm going to know He's talking to me and He's going to know He's talking to me because I've walked the walk and talked the talk. Why? Because I've looked back on the wounds and I've seen where He's brought me from and I know where He's taking me. I get excited when I think about what God has done for me. In Matthew 10:16 Jesus exhorts us "I'm sending you out like sheep among wolves. Therefore be as shrewd as snakes and as innocent as doves."

When we are going out in the world we have to be aware that there are things that are going to try to hurt us, so we have to be shrewd and we have to be cautious to avoid intentional hurts, but also like a dove, which is a representation of the Holy Spirit, a ministering spirit. We don't want to foolishly get hurt or foolishly walk into hurts but we have to be like a dove that is looking and willing to light upon somebody and minister to somebody that's hurting and if we get hurt in the process, so be it.

We not only know the Great Physician, we're working in His hospital, and we have a personal relationship with Him. You see, the nurses down at the local hospital know those doctors a whole lot better than you and I ever will because they walk with them, talk with them, work with them on a daily basis.

When things happen and I make myself vulnerable and I get hurt I can bypass the waiting room, I can bypass sitting in that exam room, I can walk right into the doctor's office and say, "Doctor, I've been hurt. I need some help" and He says, "Come on in." So we're to be as wise as serpents and as harmless as doves ministering to those that are out there.

By remembering the wounds it keeps us from busting the wounds open before they are healed and it also keeps us from getting so many new ones.

Paul says in Eph. 6:11-"Put on the full Armour of God so that you can take your stand against the devil's schemes." The only way to defeat an enemy is to know and be aware of his tricks and battle plan. Sometimes we need to remember the wounds because the devil never changes his battle plan. If he was able to defeat you with one thing he's going to come at you with it again. How do I know that? Because the same thing he beat Adam and Eve with is the same thing he's pulling today. He was able to persuade Adam and Eve that they could live independently of God's plan for their lives and he's still persuading people of the same thing today. The devil's methods have not changed. He has put different labels on them, different tags, but they are still the same.

To beat the enemy we must be aware of his schemes and his tricks. And just like God chooses to use human hands, feet and voices to accomplish His work, the devil is forced to use human hands, feet and voices to do his work also. We must study our enemy so we can come out victorious. We must look at the game films to plan not only our defense, but also our offense.

The church has been on the defensive for too long. The church has been in the retreating mode for too long. The church has been defending herself for too long. It's time for the church to go on the offensive. Why do you think that God gave us weapons of warfare that only cover our front side? (Ephesians 6:4-11) He never intended on us retreating. I've always said that if your getting your backside kicked by the enemy it's because you're facing the wrong direction.

God has given you the weapons to fight the enemy head on. So if the enemy is overtaking you, you've turned around and laid your weapons down and given him the opportunity to do it. I think it's time we learn the devil's schemes and what he's doing and pick up our weapons and go on the offensive instead of the defensive.

Let's quit worrying about offending people. The Bible says in Jeremiah 6:10b, "...*The word of the Lord is offensive to them; they find no pleasure in it*" and in I Corinthians 1:18, "*For the message of the cross is foolishness to those who are perishing, but to us who are being saved it is the power of God.*" (Emphasis added) A person that doesn't know Jesus doesn't want to be told that if they don't come into a right relationship with Jesus Christ there is a hell waiting, but that is truth. For too long we've been patting them on the back and telling them, "If you'll just come to church it will be alright," but just coming to church won't make it all right.

A healed wound, one that is healed by the Holy Spirit, is an offense to the devil and gives him a kick in the teeth. If you allow the Holy Spirit to heal you so that your wound becomes a scar, every time the devil sees it, it is a reminder to him of what God has done in your life. Every time things come and things arise you can go to this scar right here and say, "Devil, remember when you did this or this happened in my life? Well, God came and He healed it. You see this? God did this." The devil has to back away and say, "I don't want to hear that. Show me a wound; show me something that's fresh." Then you can say "No, I don't have anything fresh, but come here and we can go over the history of what God has done in my life. Where do you want to start? Do you have all day? I hope you brought a sack lunch because we're going to be here a while. Come on over, devil, let me show you what God has done." We need to remember the wounds sometimes so we can remember where God has brought us from.

You will never be effective and successful in today's battle until you remember yesterday's battle. You see the things you used yesterday to defeat the devil will work today because God gives you every weapon you will ever need in His word.

The Bible says in Luke 4:2 that Jesus was tempted for forty days not just four times, but the Bible says he was tempted for forty days. He just chose to tell us about the four. So I have to believe for forty days my Jesus was beginning to quote scripture time after time, after time. The devil would come and tempt Him with something and He would say *"It is written"* and again the devil would come and again He would say, *"It is written."*

I'm telling you, when you get depressed, *It is written*. When the enemy comes against your finances, *It is written*. When the devil comes and tells you how bad you've been, *It is written*. When your job gets rocky and the people around you hate you, *It is written*. Quoting scripture is our most powerful weapon.

I have to remember those wounds sometimes because my faith may be weak and remembering what He did for me will strengthen me. Sometimes I don't have the faith to get through this battle, but if I remember the wound that I used to have that is now a scar, I can get through this battle. I can get through this wound and I can get this healed. Then I can wear those badges of honor called scars!!

CHAPTER 5

Stories of the Scars

As we bring this book to a close there is no way I could cover this subject completely, but I trust that I have provided you with, as Jeremiah 29:11 says, "a hope and a future."

As a quick review of the last four chapters: the first chapter we talked about the fact that Scars Will Happen. If you are alive and breathing in this world, you will endure wounds.

In chapter two we talked about the Cause of the Wound, going back and finding out what exactly caused that wound so we will begin to know how to treat the wound.

In chapter three we talked about Attention to the Wound, that how you care for the wound determines the size and the ugliness of the scar.

In chapter four we talked about Remembering the Wound. Remembering the lesson that we learned, not the wound that we had incurred, but the lesson we learned through it.

Now we are going to talk about the Stories of the Scars and ministering through them. **WHEN GOD HEALS A WOUND IT IS HEALED!**

I pray that this book has set us free to be able to go out and share our stories with people so they can see that we're not perfect by human standards, we've made mistakes and we're going to share our stories. Then we're going to tell them how Jesus has forgiven us, saved us, changed us, and is daily forming us into His image and if He can do that for us He can do that for anybody.

I would dare say that if we were all truly honest and began to lay out where God has brought us from we couldn't run into anybody outside our church walls that doesn't have somebody inside our church walls that could relate to them because inside the church walls we all have scars. But let me remind you, scars are the product or the end results of a healed wound.

There is no shame in scars because that means that you were wounded and did have a hurt and now you're healed and you're moving on with God's help.

New scars can be sensitive, even painful, but you must recognize that they are healed nonetheless and as I pointed out before, a scar cannot be reopened. That would create a new wound. If God has healed you and brought you through something, that scar cannot be reopened anymore than the scar on the side of my face. The only way the enemy can do that, once God has healed a wound, is if you allow him to create a new wound, because if God has healed you, you are healed.

You might say, "I thought I was healed, but things happened that brought back a flood of emotions so I must not be healed, right?" Well I prayed and asked God about that because I know that if He has healed you, you are healed totally and completely.

Then you may ask, "Why the flood of emotions?" In the spiritual, just like the natural, with scars you can develop scar tissue. As I understand it, all scars are formed of tissue that forms the scar, but sometimes that tissue will adhere to other muscles, organs, or tissue masses forming a new bond. Then when you move a certain way, not usually a normal movement, and the adhesion formed between the scar and whatever it is attached to gets stretched it will cause pain.

Just as in the physical, so it is in the spiritual, when you are healed from those past hurts and offenses. Sometimes the scar has adhered itself to a smell, to a sound, to a taste, a feeling or something else. Let me give you an example. You are traveling and there are no music stations coming in, so you hit the scan button and it's going through scan. All of a sudden it stops on a station and BAM, there is a song that you haven't heard or thought about in years. Then suddenly these emotions come flooding in and you can remember a certain place, you can remember a certain person, a certain day or a certain event. Please understand that the memory has just adhered itself to that certain song. I have even had people tell me that if they hear the songs on the radio that they used to listen to in the bars it would bring back the intoxicating feelings. Even though they haven't drank in years and years and years. Why? Because that scar had adhered to those things. Normally these things wouldn't affect you, but when they are stretched in an unusual way it stretches the scar tissue and it hurts.

Now in the physical scar tissue heals itself most of the time. You stretch it enough and the pain disappears. Sometimes too much scar tissue forms and surgery has to be done to correct the problem. The wound is still healed, but there is just a little something in there that's an aggravation. Sometimes God will heal you of something and you have been healed, but there are things that will remind you and bring a little pain with it. Just ask God, say, "God, I need you to go in there and cut that scar tissue loose. I know you have set me free from that. I know you cleared me of that, but it's still causing me a little pain when certain things happen, so could you please take care of it?" And the Holy Spirit of God will come in and make the preparation, make the repairs or make the cuts, whatever is necessary to get you totally and completely set free from that thing. I don't believe that God needs any scar tissue in our spiritual scars.

When a person has grown up in a rough life, especially abuse situations, rape situations, and those types of situations, there are so many things that those individuals need to be healed of from that particular event. Even though they are healed sometimes just the least little thing will set them off. All of a sudden they are catapulted back by scar tissue that has adhered itself to a person, place, smell or event.

I have watched kids as I have ministered with young people, and you learn to watch these things. You will be out with a group of young people and all of a sudden you wave your hand in a gesture or motion and you see kids cower. You know immediately that you never touched them and had no intentions of touching them, but you have a real good idea of what's going on in their home life or you have a real good idea of what has happened in their life at some time. I've even seen adults react this way. You may be healed of that wound but there can still be some scar tissue that adheres itself to something. It doesn't happen all the time but sometimes it will. You might ask, "But what if it only happens now and then or once in a while? Why?"

I believe these are moments of testing. Satan realizes that the wound is healed, but if he can convince you that you're not healed then he is able to open a new wound and almost without exception, the new wound is worse than the original because now you have condemnation attached to it.

Now you have, "Oh my faith is not as strong as I thought it was. Oh I've told people that I've been healed of this. I've told people that I'm over this I've told people..." Now all of a sudden you're feeling wounded again and what you've allowed the devil to do is to come in and create a new wound. Because the condemnation is in there the wound becomes infected quickly and it will fester. It will become worse than the original.

IF GOD SAID IT IS HEALED THEN IT IS HEALED. Remember what the Bible says in Romans 8:1-*Therefore, there is now NO CONDEMNATION for those who are in Christ Jesus.* (Emphasis added) Look at these instances not as a sign of an open wound, but as a trial to see how you will react, a test if you will. Are you going to let it get you down and beat you up again? Or are you going to say, "NO, I've been healed of this and I've got the scars to prove it so I will not yield to this temptation because I AM HEALED." Yes, you feel the emotions, but it's how you react that determines the outcome. Will you stay victorious or will you let satan inflict another debilitating wound upon you? I, personally, refuse to do that because I John 4:4b tells me that, *"Greater is He that is in me than he that is in the world."*

Remember from Numbers 23:19 what the Bible says, *"God is not a man, that He should lie."* He healed me and if He said I am healed then I am healed. It doesn't matter what doctors tell me, it doesn't matter what my family or friends tell me, it doesn't matter what the little devil sitting on my shoulder sometimes tells me because God says I'm healed. You know a good swift backhand with the word of God sets that little devil on your shoulder sailing. Go ahead knock him off his perch.

Every wound brings a variety of mental, emotional, physical and spiritual pain and not all of them go away at the same time. I wish they did, just like the abuse victim, the bruises will heal, but sometimes it takes years for the emotional wounds to heal. In fact, without the help of God the emotional wound never heals.

It might be the alcoholic who comes to an altar, lays the alcohol down and gives his heart and life to Jesus Christ, but the desire is still within him. I don't understand why God doesn't just remove those desires from everybody, but I know He doesn't. The alcoholic has laid it down, but he still deals with that wound and the draw towards the alcohol.

If he will allow the Holy Spirit to come in and totally and completely work on him it will happen! If God's people will begin to show some scars and support him it will happen! It may take a little time, but it will happen because God promises us it will.

You may forgive a person, but that person continues to find new ways to offend you. It may not all go away, but you know what? Little by little and day by day that wound is getting better and your healing is happening. Things that hold you back, such as attitudes, habits or actions, just like in the natural, are not going to come to a complete stop all at once.

In the spiritual, just like in the natural, a wound causes blood and blood causes scabs. Now scabs are those ugly little things that protect a wound, while it is healing. Nobody likes to walk around with an ugly scab on a wound, but it is a sign of healing. Let me give you an example: it may be that you have prayed for forgiveness and someone you have forgiven comes up and intentionally or unintentionally rubs you the wrong way and you have to be nice to them. Now in your self it is hard to do that. There is a scab covering that wound and you haven't been completely healed, but you force yourself to be nice to that individual in the name of Jesus and the love of God. And each time you do that the scab gets a little harder and a little harder and the wound gets a little smaller and a little smaller. Then soon you can be nice to that person, smile in their face, kiss them on the cheek, and send them on their way and mean it. Why? Because the wound has healed and the scab has fallen off and now you have a scar where there was a wound. You can say, "God has healed me of that." Your feelings toward that person will be, "You can no longer open this wound. You can no longer offend me. You can no longer get joy in that because God has healed me and I have the scars to prove it."

God has really worked on me about this. He gave me a quick wit and how many of you know that if God has given you a skill or talent and you don't use it for Him, the devil will exploit it and use it?

God gave me a quick wit and when I was in the world and working in the world I was real quick to cut people down, belittle them. I was quick and I didn't care who it was or how it hurt them as long as the people around them laughed. It didn't matter to me.

The first thing God did when I got on my knees and said, "Okay God, I'm all yours; change me" was He said, "You have to change that." I said, "But God, you gave it to me." He said, "I gave and I can take away." So I find myself in situations all the time to use my quick wit and do I pass the test all the time? No, I'm sorry I don't. I try, but some people make it so easy. It's hard not to jump in there with a witty remark.

Now I find myself with opportunities to cut someone down and I have to bite my tongue. Why? Because I had a wound in there and it had a scab over it. I wanted to say something so bad it's a wonder I can still speak I had to bite my tongue so many times. I eventually got over that and I have learned to use my tongue for good and not for evil. I learned to build people up and not tear them down and that scab fell off and now I have the scar to prove it.

This will hit real close to home. You may get hurt at church. Somebody might hurt your feelings or maybe they deeply hurt you and you have to keep coming. You have a wound and a scab has formed, but each time you come that scab gets a little harder and that wound gets a little smaller.

It's hard to come because sometimes you don't want to come, lift your hands and pray. If you do, you feel guilty because you say, "I'm faking it." Well fake it for God. Sometimes it's forced and that's okay. Hebrews 13:15 says, Through Jesus, therefore, let us continually offer to God *a sacrifice of praise*—the fruit of lips that confess his name. (Emphasis added) Because as you do that, the scab gets a little harder and a little smaller and over a course of time the scab will fall off and you will be healed— that is if you don't jump and go to somebody else's church taking your wound with you. Remember sometimes you have to stop, stay where you are and let that wound heal.

If you will continue to come and let that scab get smaller and be ministered to, it will fall off. When it falls off what you're going to have is new skin and a new scar that says, "God did something for me." Those attitudes, actions and habits are just scabs, ugly little things that are covering a healing wound and they will fall off when the wound is healed.

The church wants spiritual wounds healed supernaturally, but it doesn't always happen like that. Just like in the physical, sometimes it takes a little time. Now once you're healed you have to share it!

If you had cancer and you went to a doctor that treated you like a person, made sure you got the best care, helped you through the illness and with prayer God used him to heal you, you would be quick to share it and quick to recommend that doctor. In fact, the next time you heard the word cancer come out of somebody's mouth; the next word out of your mouth would be that doctor's name.

You know what I have found? That no matter how private the illness, no matter how private the disease, when you've had a doctor who has helped you get through it, you are quick to share those experiences. Even though it's a private thing, sometimes it's something we wouldn't talk about in mixed company, but when you find somebody that is in that same situation you are quick to put a name in their hand and say, "maybe he can help you."

As a Christian it should be the same way. We know the Master Physician. He is the specialist for every need and if you meet somebody that's going through the same pain you've been through you need to introduce them to the Master Physician and be quick about it. Too many times we act like we are ashamed to recommend the Master Physician. I think it's safe to say that most Christians would recommend a doctor quicker than they would recommend Jesus. Like we talked about in the first chapter "Scars are a sign of perfection not of imperfection." Jesus is taking us from who we were to who He wants us to be. The only scars in heaven will be Jesus' scars because we will have no need for ours anymore. But right now we must be His scars to the world. We must be the signs that there are some scars in Jesus' hands and feet, some scars in Jesus' side, some scars that say He came to die for you, He's felt your pain, He knows your pain and He wants to take your pain.

We have to be Jesus' scars to them. We have to sit down and cry with them. We have to sit down and love on them. We have to sit down and share things that are painful sometimes if it means directing them to what God has done in our lives.

Some of you, I would be willing to bet, were alcoholics, but you can't talk about it in the church. Some of you were smokers and God delivered you, but we can't talk about it in the church. Paul says it like this in I Corinthians 6:9-11, "Do you not know that the wicked will not inherit the kingdom of God? Do not be deceived: *Neither the sexually immoral nor idolaters nor adulterers nor male prostitutes nor homosexual offenders nor thieves nor the greedy nor drunkards nor slanderers nor swindlers will inherit the kingdom of God. And that is what some of you were.* (Emphasis added) But you were washed, you were sanctified, you were justified in the name of the Lord Jesus Christ and by the Spirit of our God." At church we are supposed to be among our peers. We are supposed to be among people who have been delivered and lifted up. We are supposed to love and support each other.

No, we're not supposed to give the devil glory, but when an alcoholic comes in that door, I can't relate to him because I've never been there. But I can introduce him to someone who has felt his pain, someone who knows what he's going through and let him say, "Jesus walked me through this." No, we don't need to get together, like we talked about and compare scars but there has to be a time when we become vulnerable **FOR THE CAUSE OF THE CROSS**. There has to be a time when we are willing to share things that may be uncomfortable for us. We need to be willing to share things that may embarrass us a little bit. We may have to share things that will make us the "talk of the church." We have to get beyond that and let the Spirit of Almighty God come to rest on the place and if God, the creator of this universe, has forgotten it I don't care if you can remember it or not.

It doesn't matter to me what you think about me because I know what He thinks about me and He says I am cleansed, I am redeemed and I am heaven bound. What more could I share with someone than where He has brought me? I'm not proud of those things, I'm embarrassed, I'm ashamed of those things, but you know what? When I can sit down with somebody and cry and feel their pain, they know I'm real.

Whether we like it or we don't the majority of people outside the church walls think that those of us inside the church walls think we are perfect. I like the bumper sticker that says, "I'm not perfect just forgiven." It's time that people outside our walls begin to say, "We know you're not perfect and we're not perfect, but there is something in your life I need." Then we must say, "Let me introduce you to the King of kings and the Lords of lords and He can take you from where you are, He can cleanse your heart and He can heal your wounds."

We have to rise up and share some of these things; far too many of us are sitting on a gold mine that God has given us. We have to take what satan intended for evil and let God turn it into good.

Most of us are sitting on a gold mine of wealth of what God has done for us and we are afraid to share it. I'm telling you that inside these walls we should be family. My brother and I don't talk very often, but he's still my brother. He could pick up the phone today and say, "Robert, I need you to come and do something" and I would be on the road today and go do it for him. No matter what he does or where he goes he's still my brother.

Those of us inside these walls that call ourselves Christians are brothers and sisters in Christ. We love each other just the way we are. You didn't get to choose the family you were born into and maybe you don't like all your family members, but we are family through the blood of Jesus Christ and that's the way it is. We take each other with the bumps, the bruises, the scars and everything that goes with it. Why? Because we love each other through Him that loved us. (Ephesians 5:2)

Scars are our purple hearts. Purple hearts are given to those who are wounded in the line of duty, and it's a badge of honor. Most Purple Heart recipients return home to tell the stories and fight a new battle, but some of those recipients return to the front lines to resume the battle. You see in this battle we call Christianity there are no honorable discharges, there are only dishonorable discharges or promotions. When Christians pass on they get a promotion and they get to go serve with the General of all generals.

I John 4:4-"You, dear children, are from God and have overcome them, because the one who is in you is greater than the one who is in the world." We have done a great injustice in the church world because we only quote the last half of the verse, which I truly love. Now that I have begun to appreciate the first part of the verse it just opened up new area for me. It says, "You, *dear children*, are from God…"(Emphasis added) What a relief that I don't have to be a big boy in this fight, I can have childlike faith and my heavenly Father is going to come to my side. Why? Because we have already overcome them. Because greater is He that is in you than he that is in the world. Still when greater is He that is in me as a little child, I can do everything through Him who gives me strength. (Philippians 4:13)

I don't have to live with wounds. I don't have to live with people offending me. I don't have to live worrying about what the neighbor says. I don't have to worry. Why? Because greater is He that is in me than he that is in the world.

Romans 10:14 says, "How, then, can they call on the one they have not believed in? And how can they believe in the one of whom they have not heard? And how can they hear without someone preaching to them?" You are the preacher; you are the one who has to share with them.

Why do we want to share the stories of the scars? Because Revelations 12:11-"They overcame him (satan) by the blood of the Lamb and by the word of their testimony; they did not love their lives so much as to shrink from death."

What is your testimony? That's your scar!! It's your scars that say, "I was wounded, the world had beat me up, the world had me near death, but you see this scar? This is what God did for me, this is the word of my testimony," and you will overcome by the word of your testimony. In fact, if you sit back and keep it all to yourself, I will question your overcoming. Why do we have to overcome? John 16:33-"These things I have spoken unto you that ye might have peace. In the world you will have tribulation, but be of good cheer I have overcome the world."

You might say, "I don't want to share that, it makes me too uncomfortable." Then don't, but when God prompts you to share something with somebody don't be afraid to do it. *God is not going to put you in the position to share something personal that's not going to be beneficial to that one you're sharing with.* Don't be afraid to pull up your spiritual shirtsleeve a little bit and say, "See this scar. This is where God has brought me from and I am overcoming by the word of my testimony."

When things begin to go wrong, if you will begin to tell people how good God has been and is in your life, if you will begin to share, I promise you that the situation and your outlook will get better. Why? Because it's just like bragging on your Daddy and your Daddy comes to your rescue and He comes to where you are to defend you.

Unfortunately, more than once in my life I have gotten myself in a tight and I would have to call up my Dad and say, "Oh Dad, I love you, you know you're just the greatest Dad there ever was" and some of the first words out of his mouth were "Well, what do you need?" And it wasn't a condemning "what do you need?" but it was a truly, "How can I help you? What do you need?"

When I begin to brag on my Heavenly Father, when I begin to think on the good things He's done for me, it builds my faith. I know that whatever I'm involved in, whatever comes my way, I can overcome.

Now, what are some of the many benefits of overcoming?

Revelation 2:7-"He who has an ear, let him hear what the Spirit says to the churches. *To him who overcomes,* I will give the right to eat from the tree of life, which is in the paradise of God."

I want to eat from the tree of life, don't you? Adam and Eve could have eaten from it, but they chose not to. I want to eat from that tree and live forever with Jesus.

Revelation 2:11-"He who has an ear, let him hear what the Spirit says to the churches. *He who overcomes* will not be hurt at all by the second death." You and I don't have to worry if we are going to get to spend eternity with Jesus.

Revelation 2:17-"He who has an ear, let him hear what the Spirit says to the churches. *To him who overcomes*, I will give some of the hidden manna. I will also give him a white stone with a new name written on it, known only to him who receives it."

God's going to give each of you a new name that only you and Jesus will know. There will be millions and millions and millions of people there and He's going to call me by name. There's not going to be a "Hey, Robert" and seventy thousand people raise their hand. It's going to be my name that He's given me. That's worth over-coming for.

Revelation 3:5-"*He who overcomes* will, like them, be dressed in white, I will never blot out his name from the book of life, but will acknowledge his name before my Father and His angels." Sometimes when I start thinking about heaven my imagination just runs away with me. I just imagine after we are presented with a white robe, hidden manna and a stone with our new name on it that Jesus is going to take each and every one of us individually by the arm and escort us up to the Heavenly Father and say, "Father, I would like to present (insert your name). That's worth overcoming for, just think about it.

Revelation 3:21-"*To him who overcomes*, I will give the right to sit down with My Father on His throne." I don't picture this as a "come and rule with me" sharing of His throne, but I picture the Father patting His leg and saying come sit up here in my lap.

Revelation 21:7-"*He who overcomes* will inherit all this, and I will be his God and he will be my son." (Or daughter)

I can just see it now, when we go to meet Him in the air, our old body meets our new body and all those spiritual scars begin to fall off and Jesus gives us a new body that's perfect. Then we can wave good-bye to those scars because we don't need them anymore because we have overcome by the word of our testimony.

Part of our testimony is that we serve a risen Savior and not only do we serve a resurrected Savior; we ourselves have been resurrected with Him. You once were dead in your trespasses, but now you are alive in Him. You must grasp that. Not only do I serve a resurrected Savior I am a resurrected being myself. Easter means that when He came out of that grave He brought me out of that grave with Him. When I was dead in my sins and trespasses I came up out of that grave to newness of life in Him because of that we have overcome.

Even though it was dark in the middle of those wounding situations, God never left you for a moment. God may have allowed those wounds, but He never left you, and He will use those scars to His and your benefit if you will allow Him to. We have to realize and share with the world what God has done for us.

We sometimes find it hard to jump right into a salvation witness. We find it hard to just march right up to someone and say, "Do you know Jesus Christ as your personal Lord and Savior." But you know what? When you hear someone say, "I'm going through this divorce situation in my life" and you are able to say, "That's unfortunate, but I've been there too. It would have killed me if it hadn't been for the love of Jesus." Then they will say, "Oh really, what happened?" And you get the opportunity to share. Or maybe it's an abusive situation, maybe it's a financial bind situation and you get to share the goodness of how God took you through any one of those situations.

Several years ago my wife and I had our own business and I made a mistake and I didn't borrow enough money to get started. Within two years of the business being open I had floated everything I could possibly float. I had floated a lot of things personally and unfortunately I ended up ruining our credit. In the middle of that situation I cried out, " Why God? I'm a Christian, I pay my debts, and I pay people what I owe. Why am I going through this? I don't understand," and there are still things about the situation that I don't understand. But I do know this. Had that business jumped on its feet immediately and went into a full run and been very profitable I probably wouldn't be in the ministry today. Had things not gone wrong, had I not gone through the financial struggles, I wouldn't have been willing to say, "Ok God, it's all yours" and let it go. He let me keep the business for three more years. It was up and running and at one point I had 5 employees, doing warranty work for 30 different companies, had a good reputation in the town;

things were going good. Then God said, "Ok now it's time to close it up."

So, on October 31, 2000, we locked the doors on it and walked away from it. I was making $250 a week as a youth pastor and my wife was not working outside the home. We had a $700 a month house payment, two daughters in private Christian school, it was two months before Christmas and you know what happened? We went through Christmas and never charged one single Christmas present. We went through Christmas and never missed a house payment and our girls stayed in private school. I don't know how, but I do know that now when I sit down with people with financial problems and we begin to talk I can say, "You may have to walk through this, but God will walk through it with you. And if you will allow Him to, here is what can happen, here's what can happen on the other side, here's what can be beneficial to you." But that takes guts because I have to put my pride down and I have to admit to something that happened in my life that I'm not real proud of.

Guess what has happened since then? That has been less than seven years at the time of this writing and to show you how good God is, my wife and I will soon be buying our third house. Yes, our financial struggles still show up on every credit report, but God has taken something that was bad and He turned it around because of obedience. It's hard to share that, but I'm willing to share that scar if it will help somebody realize that God is Faithful.

So my challenge to you is to find opportunities where you can share what God has done for you. It may be a wound that has scarred you deeply, or it may be one you have to go looking for to find, but when God opens up the opportunity for you to share something personal in your life of how He has brought you through something, be willing to step through that at whatever the cost or the pain to overcome so someone can come to the saving grace of Jesus Christ.

We are not going to win our cities with our music. We are not going to win our cities with our children's ministries although that will be beneficial getting them in the door. We're not going to win our cities with our youth ministries. We're not going to win our cities with our preaching. We're going to win our cities as we start to become real with people and they see that there are real people inside the church walls and we love them with the love of Jesus.

Then they will come in the doors; then the music will impact them; then the preaching will impact them; then the children's ministry will impact them; then the youth ministry will impact them. We're never going to get them in the door if they don't see the love of Jesus shining through us. My heart really burns for the lost and as I walk these streets, as I walk through stores and businesses, I see on people's faces the agony, the pain, the hurting and the obviousness that they don't know the love of Jesus in their lives. And should Jesus come, most likely they would spend eternity in a devil's hell – that breaks my heart. We've become too calloused inside our walls, we've become too used to seeing hurting people and not feeling anything. We've become too comfortable with our church club that we have to lift the unwritten membership restrictions and open the doors and just like Jesus say, **"WHOSOEVER WILL, SEE MY SCARS."**

CPSIA information can be obtained
at www.ICGtesting.com
Printed in the USA
LVHW08s1619210718
584530LV00001B/34/P

9 781597 814805